John and Wendy Jones, 24 ix 1997

# The Attack on Taranto

# The Attack on Taranto

*Blueprint for Pearl Harbor*

Thomas P. Lowry
*and*
John W. G. Wellham

STACKPOLE
BOOKS

Published by
STACKPOLE BOOKS
5067 Ritter Road
Mechanicsburg, PA 17055

Map on p. vii by J. F. W. Pembridge

Printed in the United States of America

10   9   8   7   6   5   4   3   2   1

First edition

**Library of Congress Cataloging-in-Publication Data**
    Lowry, Thomas P. (Thomas Power), 1932–
      The attack on Taranto : blueprint for Pearl Harbor / Thomas P. Lowry and John W. G. Wellham. — 1st ed.
        p.    cm.
    Includes bibliographical references and index.
    ISBN 0-8117-1726-7
      1. Taranto, Battle of, 1940.   I. Wellham, John W. G.   II. Title.
D756.5.T37L69   1995
940.54'21755—dc20                          95-10618
                                              CIP

# Contents

➤

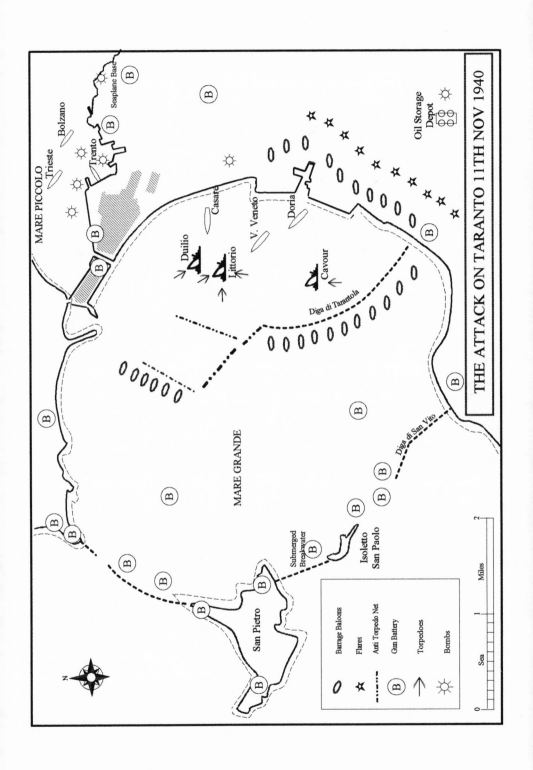

THE ATTACK ON TARANTO 11TH NOV 1940

Oil Storage
Depot

MARE PICCOLO

Trieste

Bolzano

Seaplane Base

Trento

Casare

Duilio

Littorio

V. Veneto

Doria

Cavour

Diga di Tarantola

MARE GRANDE

Diga di San Vito

Submerged
Breakwater

Isoletto
San Paolo

San Pietro

N

Barrage Baloons

Flares

Anti Torpedo Net

Gun Battery

Torpedoes

Bombs

0    Sea    1    Miles    2

# Foreword

➤

BEFORE THE CHICKEN CAME THE EGG, AND JUST AS SURELY BEFORE PEARL Harbor came Taranto—the little-remembered British carrier-borne attack against the Italian fleet at anchor at its Mediterranean base on November 11, 1940.

Twenty-one shaky-looking, double-winged torpedo bombers, appropriately named Stringbags, struggle off the deck of the carrier *Illustrious* (the *Eagle* having been withdrawn for repairs at the eleventh hour) and ascend to between 4,000 and 7,000 feet. Unflinchingly, they drive toward the Italian coast.

Lacking radar, the Italian naval base at Taranto is protected by new-fangled sonic listening devices that can detect an aircraft engine many miles distant. With the aid of these contraptions, the Italians, unlike their better-equipped American counterparts at Pearl Harbor, quickly spot the oncoming intruders and fling up every jagged piece of hot metal they can muster. Most of the Stringbags make it through the lethal hail, descend to wave-scraping altitude, and loose their weapons.

Furiously firing, the Italian gunners pump up nearly 30,000 projectiles at the assailants. Many are hit, and two are felled. One crippled Stringbag has to endure a further blast of hot metal when it attempts to land on the *Illustrious* without properly identifying itself.

When the sea spray settles, the dreadnaught *Cavour,* the battleships *Littorio* and *Duilio,* and several lesser warships are either sunk or heavily damaged. Shore facilities are in flames.

Among those paying close attention to these events is the Japanese admiral Isoroku Yamamoto, soon to become the architect of the Pearl Harbor attack. So fascinated is Yamamoto that he orders full reports on the Taranto attack from both the Japanese naval attaché in Berlin and his tactical air chief, Minoru Genda, who is in London. Six months later, a whole delegation of Japanese brass inspects Taranto.

Is Yamamoto influenced by Taranto? Well, as they say, is the Pope Catholic?

The Taranto raid was important because it was, as the authors of this superb account declare in their subtitle, a "blueprint for Pearl Harbor." And Pearl Harbor, after all, is worth thinking and writing about because it may have been the most important single event of the century now drawing to a close.

The Japanese surprise attack was the event that brought the United States, kicking and screaming, into the Second World War, which was very largely an extension of the First World War. It started a conflict that led to the Age of Nuclear Weapons, and it brought the United States to the center of the world stage—a position from which it has not yet retreated.

Thus any knowledge that we can gather about such a momentous happening is well worth having, and this Captain Lowry and Commander Wellham have given us in good measure in what must be a definitive account of the Taranto raid. The dramatic story of the raid is particularly well told, because Commander Wellham actually took part in the attack.

The reader may ask, Did Taranto, as well, have a precursor? The authors tackle this hotly debated question as bravely as the Stringbag pilots of whom they write, explaining that British strategists, as well as Yamamoto, were influenced by such military intellectuals as Hector C. Bywater and by a number of war games carried out as far back as the 1920s.

*The Attack on Taranto* is an authoritative document of human heroism that provides us with a heart-in-mouth description of the actual raid. One shudders as one reads of flaming tracer bullets ripping through the canvas wings.

And surely one can sympathize with the Stringbag pilot who, when asked how he felt about returning to the firestorm over Taranto for a second raid the next night, replied, "After all, they only asked the Light Brigade to do it once!"

William H. Honan
National Higher Education Correspondent
*The New York Times*

# Preface

➤

ALL BATTLES ARE DESTRUCTIVE, BUT A FEW ARE ALSO PRODUCTIVE. SUCH a battle is one in which the war in progress is moved a significant step toward resolution. The most productive military encounter is one in which the largest step toward ending the war is combined with a minimal loss of life.

History is full of examples of military events that had no long-term benefits and yet were the cause of great slaughter. Grant's Cold Harbor campaign, the Crimean War, and the Japanese invasion of China are certainly examples of unproductivity and of great bloodshed, which led only to inconclusive stalemate and exhaustion, with neither the participants nor their heirs receiving any useful reward. In current jargon, they had a very poor "cost-benefit ratio."

There are some noncombat military events that have had great impact. The cracking of the Enigma codes, the installation of radar in England in 1939, and Stalin's purge of his own best officers are examples of decisive events far removed from the field of battle.

But in war itself, productive events—those that make a real difference, with minimal loss of life—are precious few. And of these few, the raid at Taranto may be the shining star, a moment when a handful of men, with boldness and precision, shaped the course of events for generations yet unborn.

In the writing of history, there are two major styles: macrohistory and microhistory.

The former focuses on the long view—on grand strategy and on geopolitics. The authors of macrohistory paint with a broad brush upon a great canvas. Their maps show huge arrows, spheres of influence, the movements of armies. They use sweeping and inclusive phrases, such as "The Soft Underbelly of Europe" and "The War to End All Wars."

At the other end of the scale are the microhistorians. In the technical arena, they are best represented by the American Civil War buffs, who publish books on the variations in canteen design and sword blade embellishment. The personal microhistorians, either from firsthand experience or vicariously, describe wars bullet by bullet, foxhole by foxhole. Their broadest view is the next tree, the next ridge. Their theme is personal survival, individual pain, moment-by-moment events, the incoherence, confusion, and blindness of combat itself.

Yet there is no inherent conflict between the macrohistorians and their more narrowly focused counterparts. All wars have some raison d'être, some underlying strategy, whether brilliant or stupid, far-seeing or myopic. The strategists always have some concept as the foundation of action. And after all the great circles and arrows are drawn on war room maps, the actual reality of battle is men with skin only a millimeter thick, their bodies packed with vital organs, fragile creatures, dependent wholly upon the five quarts of blood they carry into combat. The immediate personal risk is theirs; their imperative goal is to stay alive another minute and, having achieved that, to continue this process in the minutes to come.

In this narrative, we have tried to blend the why and the how of great strategic problems with the immediacy and factual detail of those who lived those events, in the knowledge and humility that one of us has been spared such perils in his own life and the other has survived them.

# Acknowledgments

➤

THIS BOOK PROGRESSED FROM PENCILED SCRIBBLE TO A NEAT AND FINISHED manuscript through the efforts of Beverly A. Lowry, who typed three successive versions. Words cannot express our thanks.

William C. Davis and Sylvia Frank saw the possibilities of the first version and, with skilled hands, guided us to a more coherent presentation of these historic events.

We are deeply grateful to the many people whose professional experience has helped us with this book, sharing with us both their personal encounters and their archival treasures. Not necessarily in the order of their contribution, we would like to take special notice of the following contributors:

In the United Kingdom, Comdr. G. R. M. Going DSO OBE Royal Navy (ret.), Comdr. S. Bramley Royal Navy RN Staff College, Mr. C. Gadd, Group Capt. J. F. W. Pembridge AFC RAF, Comdr. D. G. J. Wilkey CBE DSC VRD RNR (ret.), Dr. D. G. Chandler RMA Sandhurst, Group Capt. S. A. Wrigley RAF, Mr. C. M. Hobson RAF Staff College; Mr. David Richardson, Ms. Eunice Matthews, and Mr. Graham Mottram, of the Fleet Air Arm Museum; Mr. N. B. Travers RAF Museum; and Ms. A. E. Duffield, Mr. A. Williams, and Mr. P. Kemp, of the Imperial War Museum.

In the United States, Mr. Bob Diemert, Mr. Frederick A. Johnson of the USAF Flight Test Center, Mr. Henry Sakaida, Mr. Richard S. Lowry, Mr. Michael Walker of the U.S. Naval Historical Center, Mr. James R. Arthur of the Center for Air Force History, Mr. Bruce Smith of the Admiral Nimitz Center, Ms. Patty M. Maddocks of the U.S. Naval Institute, Mr. John J. Slonaker of the U.S. Army Military History Institute, Mr. Archie DiFante of the U.S. Air Force Historical Research Agency; and Mr. Robert Mikesh, Mr. Cliff Banyas, Mr. Kenton A. Sandine, and Ms. Christine Caskie of the National Air and Space Museum.

*Chapter One*

➤

# The Curtain Rises

Since man first went to sea, he has sought safe harbors. Since he first went to war in ships, those ports became vital to sustaining his fleets. Catch an enemy's fleet in harbor, destroy the ships and dock facilities, and a bold attacker could win a war. Two such vital anchorages, Taranto and Pearl Harbor, are separated by 12,000 miles of oceans and continents, yet war united them in the deadliest of brotherhoods.

Taranto is a port in southern Italy, lying in the arch of the boot of the Italian peninsula, 250 miles southeast of Rome. Founded in 706 B.C. as a Spartan Greek trading post called Taras, it was known as Tarantum in the years of the Roman Empire. Its fine natural harbor has been improved over the millenia by the addition of breakwaters and elaborate docking facilities. Pearl Harbor, on the other hand, has no such ancient origins. This great naval facility in Hawaii, the final jumping-off place into the vastness of the central Pacific Ocean, was blasted and dredged out of a shallow lagoon and marshy area in the late 1920s. Both harbors adjoin major cities; in 1940, both Honolulu and Taranto had populations around 200,000.

Each harbor was a powerful threat to the fleets of an opponent. In 1941, the U.S. Pacific Fleet at Pearl Harbor was the major barrier to Japanese plans to expand its empire south and east. In 1940, Taranto housed most of the Italian fleet and stood almost astride the sea lanes that linked British interests in Gibraltar, Egypt, and on to India and Singapore.

To launch an attack on either harbor posed major problems for the aggressor. The Japanese needed to cross 4,000 miles of open ocean, undetected, with no resupply available, and attack a harbor defended by the guns of sixty-eight warships, various shore batteries, and more than 100 fighter planes. The British needed to approach Italy, through the confined waters of the Mediterranean, undetected by dozens of Italian reconnaissance planes, and survive the gunfire of fifty-four warships, twenty-one shore batteries of four-inch guns, and numerous batteries of rapid-fire guns, while dodging the steel cables of sixty antiaircraft barrage balloons. Several squadrons of fighter planes sat poised at Taranto, ready to rise and meet any attacker.

It was not as though there were no precedents for successful attacks upon fleets in harbor. Naval bases anticipate attack and, depending on the historical era, have had a variety of active defenses, ranging from the catapults and muzzle-loading cannons of the past to the projected, but unbuilt, Star Wars defenses against ballistic missiles. Passive defenses, too, have been important: giant chains, mines, and antisubmarine nets, for example. At the Battle of Salamis in 480 B.C., the Greeks altered history by crushing a Persian fleet. In 413 B.C., Gyllipus destroyed an Athenian fleet in Syracuse harbor. In A.D. 1340, Edward III of England destroyed a French invasion fleet in Sluys. In 1567, Sir Francis Drake destroyed a Spanish fleet at Cadiz, using fire ships, thus "singeing the King of Spain's beard." In 1666, De Ruyter destroyed the English fleet at anchor in the Medway. In 1759, Adm. Sir Edward Hawke destroyed a French fleet trapped in Quiberon Bay. From the late Renaissance until around 1880, shore batteries of muzzle-loading cannons guarded the principal harbors of Europe, and the ships within were often safe—but not always.

In 1798, Lord Horatio Nelson destroyed the French fleet at anchor in Aboukir Bay.

In 1800, in yet another shift of alliances in Napoleonic Europe, the Russians, Danes, Norwegians, Swedes, and Prussians formed the Armed Neutrality of the North and showed signs of an alliance with Napoleon.

Lord Nelson, under the ineffectual Sir Hyde Parker, was sent to demonstrate to the Danes the unwisdom of such a course. In the attack on Copenhagen, Nelson avoided the more usual passage into the harbor, as it was heavily fortified, and chose the outer channel, with its shoaling problems and difficult winds, bringing the Danes to battle without receiving the initial heavy pounding intended for him by the great guns of the Trekroner Fortress. Nelson's unorthodox approach set the stage for victory.

The Napoleonic Wars also held numerous examples of small-scale actions, "cutting out" expeditions, in which a single ship might enter a harbor (or send in small boats with muffled oars), usually by night or in bad weather, evade the shore batteries through poor visibility or diversionary actions, and sail captured enemy ships out of the very harbors meant to protect them.

With the invention of long-range rifled cannon, such exploits became less possible. Scout planes and the new coastal defense guns created danger for any ship within twenty miles of the land. The bombing demonstrations of Billy Mitchell in the 1920s suggested that aircraft could do more than just scout, though Mitchell's enthusiasm outran the technology of his day.

In 1939, the British Fleet lay in "impregnable" Scapa Flow; the U-47 penetrated those defenses and sank the *Royal Oak*.

In April 1940, Fleet Air Arm Skua dive-bombers sank the German cruiser *Koenigsberg,* the first major warship destroyed in combat by aircraft. The element of surprise and the lack of effective German air cover were essential ingredients in this British success, one of the few bright spots in the disastrous failures of the defense of Norway.

The transition in harbor attacks from surface engagement to aerial assault may be seen at Mers-el-Kebir, a North African port near Oran, where the French fleet lay in late June 1940. France had surrendered to Germany; Hitler promised not to use the French fleet, but few believed him. In one of the most distasteful events of the war, Admiral Somerville was instructed to advise his French counterpart that if he did not surrender the French ships at Mers-el-Kebir (four capital ships and six destroyers), he would be attacked. In the simplest terms, the French refused and the British fired. Three of the great ships were badly damaged, but a fourth, the battle cruiser *Strasbourg,* escaped from the harbor only to be attacked by Swordfish torpedo planes from the *Ark Royal*. The aerial pursuit was unsuccessful, but it set the stage for aviation's role in future harbor assaults.

The day after the attack, a French admiral announced that the *Dunquerque,* which had beached herself, had "minimal" damage and would soon be repaired. The British took note of this announcement, and on July 6, three waves of Fleet Air Arm torpedo planes blasted the *Dunquerque* into unrepairable wreckage.

The following month, August 1940, saw the British attack upon four Italian naval vessels in Bomba Harbor on the Libyan coast. In a few minutes, three Swordfish biplanes torpedoed and sank all four Italian ships. No British surface vessels were involved in this remarkable event.

Yet no attempt had ever been made upon harbor facilities of such magnitude as Taranto and Pearl Harbor, protected by such an array of defenses. Taranto would be the first on the stage of history since, in 1940, it was Britain that was at war, while America still slumbered, wrapped in its warm cocoon of isolationism and self-complacency.

The solution to successfully attacking each of these maritime fortresses rested, in the final analysis, on a single commander. Command—in particular, military command—has its responsibilities. No matter how many junior officers may offer information and advice, the man at the top carries the final weight on his shoulders, and on his shoulders alone.

The career of HMS *Glorious* illustrates that bravery is not enough in war, but that eternal vigilance and anticipation of events is the ever-present duty of command; a single lapse in a commander's attention can yield a harsh outcome indeed in the unforgiving equations of war.

The war began on September 1, 1939. Hitler and Stalin crushed Poland in days and divided the corpse. Then came the ominous silence of the sitzkrieg, which lasted 189 days.

At 5:00 in the morning on April 9, 1940, the German ambassador to Norway handed the Norwegian foreign minister, Dr. Koht, a note demanding immediate surrender. Since there had been no war, Dr. Koht rejected the note and the opportunity to surrender.

German ships lying off the 1,200 miles of Norwegian coastline, dispatched there days before, launched a dawn assault on the ports of Arendal, Stavanger, Bergen, Kristiansand, Trondheim, and Narvik, as Nazi parachutists descended on the same ports on a double envelopment. Within hours, every important port was in German hands. The only Norwegian success came when the guns and torpedoes of the old fortress at Oscarsborg, on the route to Oslo, sank two German ships, the *Bluecher* and the *Brummer,* but everywhere else there was defeat.

The initial British response came five days later, when 1,500 troops were landed near Trondheim. Sent without a single antiaircraft gun, a single piece of artillery, or air cover, they were chewed to pieces by the Germans. This disastrous bit of high command incompetence was relieved briefly by the victory of the *Warspite,* which sank seven German destroyers at Narvik. But this was not enough. By June 7, only seven weeks after being landed, the British soldiers in Norway were ordered withdrawn.

HMS *Glorious* started life in 1917 as a battle cruiser, with fifteen-inch guns. In 1924, she entered the yard and was stripped of her turrets and superstructure. When she emerged and entered service in 1930, she was an aircraft carrier, with a 570-foot flight deck, capable of thirty-two knots with full steam. Her normal complement was thirty-six aircraft. In 1939, she initially carried twelve Sea Gladiators and thirty-six Swordfish.

In the brief Norwegian campaign, the *Glorious* and another British aircraft carrier, the *Ark Royal,* played a part. The *Glorious*'s first action was to deliver eighteen RAF Gladiator biplanes to Norway. These were flown off April 24 to a "base" on a frozen lake. There were insufficient mechanics and not enough spare parts for such an operation. Fuel was delivered in four-gallon tins, carried on sleds. The Germans bombed the lake, breaking up the ice. Within forty-eight hours, only one of the original eighteen Gladiators was still operational.

On May 26, the *Glorious* returned to deliver eighteen Hawker Hurricanes; this time they had terra firma on which to land. But May 26 was also the first day of the Dunkirk evacuation. British forces were needed at home. The *Ark Royal* and *Glorious* were to cover the retreat from Norway. It was decided to fly the RAF Gladiators onto the aircraft carriers and to destroy the Hurricanes, since it was believed that Hurricanes could not be landed on the small deck of a carrier, but Squadron Leader Kenneth B. B. Cross requested permission to try. The evening of June 7, the two carriers turned into the wind and put on twenty-six knots. Three Hurricanes, with their tires slightly deflated to facilitate braking, landed safely.

Based on this success, early the next morning twenty-two more planes were landed on *Glorious:* eight Gladiators, ten Hurricanes, and two Walrus amphibians.

That same day, the *Glorious,* short of fuel, steamed directly for England, escorted by the destroyers *Ardent* and *Acasta*. The *Ark Royal,* with a better fuel supply, accompanied by nineteen other ships, took a more northerly route to lessen the chance of German detection.

At 3:45 that afternoon, the lookout on the *Glorious* saw the masts of two large warships rise over the horizon to the south. They were not British.

Capt. G. D'Oyly-Hughes, commanding officer of the *Glorious,* had not flown off any reconnaissance planes to scout his path. (The *Ark Royal,* on the other hand, sent ahead of her path Skuas, Swordfish, and even Walrus flying boats, fully on the alert for German planes, ships, and submarines.)[1] He did not have his engines ready to provide full speed.

Certainly he had his reasons. His pilots were very tired. To fly off planes would have meant turning 180 degrees, heading north into the wind, and losing time and fuel. Only one of his Swordfish was fully serviceable. Having all boilers ready for use would have used extra fuel. Whatever the reasons, however, these were grievous errors. Before sundown, his pilots were dead, his precious, rescued Hurricanes settling to the bottom of the North Sea.

The masts on the horizon had belonged to the German battle cruisers *Gneisenau* and *Scharnhorst,* both equipped with the latest radar gun control.

Each mounted nine eleven-inch guns, and each opened fire at 4:30 P.M. at a range of 28,000 yards.

The *Glorious* turned to run. D'Oyly-Hughes ordered full steam and tried to launch a few planes, but not a single plane could be flown off, as salvo after salvo ripped through the hull and deck of the *Glorious*. None of the three British ships had guns that could reach the Germans. One of the first salvos had destroyed most of the *Glorious*'s radio equipment, and she was able to send just one low-power message, received only by HMS *Devonshire,* too far away to help. They were completely helpless.

Forty-five minutes had passed between first sighting and the first salvo. What if Captain D'Oyly-Hughes had had his Swordfish fueled up and ready to fly off with torpedoes, or with armor-piercing bombs? What if he had had steam up? The *Glorious* was capable of thirty-two knots under good conditions; the *Scharnhorst* could do just twenty-seven knots. Could the *Glorious* have gone north, into the wind, stayed out of gun range, launched her planes, and radioed for assistance before running out of fuel? Could the *Ark Royal* have come within Swordfish range? (The Germans had no air cover.) But this is only speculation.

At 5:20 P.M., the *Glorious,* burning violently, was abandoned, just as the *Ardent* was blown to pieces. The *Acasta* had no hope of survival but, in an aggressive final stroke, managed to put one torpedo into the *Scharnhorst,* which destroyed two of the three engine rooms. But that was all. An hour after the *Glorious,* the *Acasta* too went to the bottom.

*Acasta* had one survivor, plucked from the sea by the *Gneisenau.* Seven survivors of the *Glorious* and *Ardent* were picked up by a German seaplane.

After three days on the freezing water, thirty-eight more survivors, including Squadron Leader Cross, were rescued by a Norwegian vessel. Dozens of men who had not been killed in the shelling died of exposure that night in the black subarctic waters.

The bravery and skill of the pilots was for naught when, through poor planning, they were unable to fly and perform the job for which they had been trained. The British losses in three hours consisted of three ships, 1,515 men, and thirty-five combat aircraft. The best defense for an aircraft carrier is its own aircraft, and the neglect of this principle can be fatal. The flight deck of the *Glorious* had been littered with rescued airplanes. Could more of them have been lowered to the hangar deck below? Could some of them have been parked farther to the side, or even thrown into the sea, discarding the precious rescued craft in favor of an even more important goal—that of keeping a functional launching space? Could some way have been found to preserve the *Glorious's* function as a combat-ready carrier rather than leaving her as a passive transport craft, a mere ferry boat?

A commander, no matter how fatigued, must be vigilant; no matter how perplexed, must be analytic; no matter how set upon, must be steadfast. Captain D'Oyly-Hughes failed. What would be the fate of men with even wider responsibilities?

In the late summer of 1940, the two commanders most concerned with Taranto and Pearl Harbor were Andrew B. Cunningham and Isoroku Yamamoto.

# Chapter Two

➢

# Two Worried Admirals

IN THE SUMMER OF 1940, THERE WERE TWO WORRIED ADMIRALS. THEY were of different nationalities, spoke different languages, commanded greatly different fleets, and faced very different dilemmas, but the scope and intensity of their problems were similar, and failure for either would mean disaster.

One admiral, Sir Andrew B. Cunningham, commander in chief of the British Mediterranean Fleet, was responsible for keeping open the sea lanes to the Suez Canal. In the 1,600 miles from Gibraltar to Suez, the only friendly port that summer was Malta, a tiny island devoid of resources and under almost constant bombardment by the Italian Air Force. The long sea passage was constricted in its midsection, the narrows between Tunisia and Sicily. Constant surveillance by Italian submarines and long-range aircraft assured that any British supply convoy would be detected and brought under attack. Since the cargo ships of that day could rarely exceed twelve knots, days would pass before they were beyond the range of enemy bombers.

The defense of the Suez Canal was the key to keeping the Axis powers away from the rich oil fields of the Persian Gulf. The loss of the Suez would also disrupt passage to India, Singapore, and Australia, forcing British ships to sail an extra 10,000 miles around South Africa.

Facing Cunningham was a much larger and more modern Italian fleet, based in Taranto and other home ports, with no supply-line problems at all, squarely astride the Gibraltar-Suez passage. Taranto's location in the south of Italy placed it conveniently close to the British Malta-to-Suez run, yet sequestered enough in the Gulf of Taranto to be easily guarded by land-based planes. Taranto had a superb protected anchorage three miles across and an inner harbor with extensive docking, repair, and aviation facilities, and it was one of the most heavily fortified harbors

9

in the world, with dozens of antiaircraft batteries, searchlights, and listening devices.

How, with an aging fleet in desperate need of repairs and cut off from supplies, could Cunningham defeat a larger and more modern navy operating from its own coastline and fortified harbors? This was Cunningham's dilemma.

The other admiral was Isoroku Yamamoto, commander in chief of the Combined Fleet of the Imperial Japanese Navy, a post he had held since August 1939. He saw clearly that Japan was on a collision course with the United States. Japan had been bogged down for years in a land war in mainland China, and although Japan had secured oil and wheat from Manchuria and rice from China, this hardly counterbalanced the international ill will the country had generated by its atrocities against the Chinese people. The United States brought pressure to bear upon Japan, restricting the supply of oil and steel.

The rocky islands of the Land of the Rising Sun are almost totally lacking in natural resources, and the rich oil, tin, and rubber supplies of Southeast Asia and the Dutch East Indies were irresistible. But it was also clear that an invasion of Southeast Asia would bring the United States into the war, and Yamamoto, who had been the naval attaché at the Japanese embassy in Washington, D.C., from 1926 to 1928, knew the enormous latent industrial strength of the United States.

He understood all too well that when the steel of Indiana, the corn of Illinois, the oil of Texas, the vehicle assembly lines of Michigan, the shipyards of Washington and Maryland, and the aircraft builders of California were harnessed to a war effort, they could and would crush Japan.

What stood between Japan and quick victory was the U.S. Pacific Fleet. If it could be destroyed in the first moments of the war, Yamamoto believed, then Japan would be master of half the globe. Destroying a major fleet is no easy task, but to fail in that destruction meant, in Yamamoto's thinking, certain defeat for Japan. He must succeed. But how? This was Yamamoto's worry.

Who were these men, entrusted by their nations with such awesome responsibility? Andrew B. Cunningham was known also by the nickname of ABC. Cunningham's father was a professor of anatomy at Trinity College, Dublin, but young ABC had no interest in medicine. From his earliest years, he favored the sea, spending as many hours as he could in sailboats, and entering the Royal Navy training ship *Britannia* as a cadet in 1897. When he completed his training two years later, he was tenth out of a class of sixty-five.

He was just in time for action in the Boer War and served on the front lines with a mobile naval gun detachment. A few years later, he was back in England in sublieutenant courses, receiving top marks in seamanship and torpedo. He then served, from 1903 to 1907, as second in command of the destroyer *Locust,* under a lieutenant with a reputation for getting rid of sublieutenants who failed to meet his standards. ABC did well, and he developed a great fondness for service in destroyers and the other swift, lightly armored craft whose responsiveness and rapid maneuverability (and great tendency to induce seasickness) either exhilarated or exhausted those who served aboard them.

The close quarters of small ships were ideal for ABC, who combined warmth, humor, generosity, and sympathy with a demand for the utmost in excellence and endurance. He was given command of the destroyer *Scorpion,* where he worked his way through eleven sublieutenants before settling on a man he liked and trusted.

Cunningham served at the disastrous Dardanelles Campaign in World War I and noted well the sad results of poor coordination between navy and army forces. He also noted well the effectiveness of England's first carrier-based air strike, launched at dawn on July 19, 1918. Seven Sopwith Camels flew off HMS *Furious* and bombed the German zeppelin base at Tondern. These tiny planes, using fifty-pound bombs, destroyed two enormous hangars filled with airships. (The Royal Navy's ambivalence about aviation was reflected in the design of the *Furious:* The foredeck was flat, the afterdeck built like a battleship, with turrets. A plane could take off, but there was no way it could land.)

Cunningham's superiors saw his capacities as an effective leader, aggressive fighter, and highly competent seaman, who still kept the human qualities that had caused him to be criticized as a cadet for "laughing in study" and "skylarking at muster." He served in the Channel warfare, then off the coast of Latvia, and returned to Istanbul in 1923, during the political turmoil in Turkey.

Through the 1930s, he steadily advanced, with staff jobs, command of the battleship *Rodney,* service as aide-de-camp to the king in 1932, and command of the destroyer flotillas in the Mediterranean from 1933 to 1937. In this position, he pushed for fleet readiness, with special attention to night torpedo attack, sensing the increasing danger of the growing Italian fleet and its menacing, posturing master, Benito Mussolini. In 1937, the sudden illness of Admiral Sir Geoffrey Blake gave Cunningham the combined posts of commander of the battle cruiser squadron and second in command of the Mediterranean fleet with the *Hood* as his flagship.

As war approached, Cunningham was called back to London. He protested that he had no talent for paperwork, but the Board of Admiralty had such confidence in him that he was given the post of deputy sea lord, doing the actual work of the first sea lord, who had fallen ill. Later, Cunningham's experience in the upper reaches of bureaucracy, combined with his own forceful character, enabled him to say no to Churchill on occasions when the prime minister's ideas on how to run the war outstripped practical realities.

In June 1939, to ABC's great relief, he was at sea again, back in the Mediterranean area, with the post of commander in chief, Mediterranean Station, and his admiral's flag hoisted on the battleship *Warspite*.[1] Here he faced a great challenge. The British military forces, in all branches, had been starved for funds for decades, both through the policies of men like Neville Chamberlain, who hoped to mollify Hitler by not rearming, and by the privation of the Great Depression, which had impoverished nearly all the nations of the world. But ABC had the loyal following of his men and the experience of forty-one years of active naval service.

Within a year, Cunningham's full task was at hand. In May 1940, the Nazis defeated France and pushed the British into the sea at Dunkirk, where in the first week of June, a third of a million men staggered across the beaches into small craft, destroyers, and transports and were carried to Britain. This bittersweet disaster and triumph left the British Army largely intact but without its equipment, which remained on the sands of Dunkirk. In the air, the Germans began their bombing of Britain in preparation for an invasion across the Channel.

Disaster followed disaster. In June 1940, the Italians had 300,000 troops in Cyrenaica, along the Libyan-Egyptian border, equipped with 1,800 field guns and 339 tanks. The early September invasion of Egypt penetrated sixty miles in four days. Fortunately for the 30,000 British and Empire troops, outnumbered ten to one, the Italians stopped at Sidi Barrâni and dug in.

With the British Army out of action and the Germans entering Paris, the Italians struck across the French border, losing 7,000 troops and failing to capture the French Riviera. Though the Italian attack on France in itself had small military significance, it brought Italy into the war officially, its modernized fleet now in direct confrontation with Cunningham.[2]

On the opposite side of the globe, Admiral Yamamoto had also been preparing many years for the task ahead. In 1904, when the Russo-

Japanese War began, Yamamoto was in his third year at the Naval Academy on Eta Jima. Preparations for war, unknown to the Japanese public, had begun in the preceding October, when Vice Admiral Heihachirō Togō had been given command of the fleet and was told to ready it for an attack on Russia.

Japan, just emerging as an industrial nation after centuries of medieval isolation, could not risk damage to its fleet and, further, had to destroy the Russian Pacific Fleet before the Russians could prevent Japan from moving its army to the mainland. Togo concluded that a surprise attack, before declaring war, was the proper answer.

On the night of February 8, 1904, the Russian fleet lay anchored at Port Arthur. The officers were ashore at a fancy dress ball, while outside, the dark waters of the Gulf of Po Hai were lashed by an icy storm. At midnight, a flotilla of Japanese destroyers entered the harbor and fired salvos of torpedoes into the sleeping ships. The Russians lost two of their newest battleships and their best cruiser. Midshipman Yamamoto, still at the Naval Academy, was thrilled by Togo's triumph.[3]

Eighteen months later, his excitement reached fever pitch when, as a cadet aboard Togo's flagship *Mikasa,* he participated in the battle of Tsushima Strait. This decisive fight, which annhilated the Russian fleet and won the war, confirmed in Yamamoto his admiration of Togo and his determination to subordinate everything—his friendships, even his family life—to his destiny in what he regarded as Japan's historic mission. Young Yamamoto had lost two fingers off his left hand during the Battle of the Japan Sea, when he was serving aboard the *Nisshan* and one of its guns burst during firing. Yamamoto regarded this loss as a small price to pay for meeting with his destiny and following in the footsteps of his hero.

On the eve of Tsushima, Togo had signaled to his battle fleet, "The rise or fall of the nation is at stake in this battle," using Naval Code Z. The letter *Z* and what it meant to Yamamoto in the years ahead was to have historic significance.

Yamamoto's determination and intelligence assured a steady progression in his career. After the First World War, from 1919 to 1921, he studied at Harvard University. From 1926 to 1928 he served as naval attaché at Washington, D.C., where he devoted himself to the strategic concepts of the U.S. Navy rather than the narrower tactical considerations that preoccupied his colleagues. He also perfected his poker game, at which, according to his U.S. Office of Naval Intelligence file, he was a "habitual winner." It was also noted that he was Go champion of the Imperial Navy, as well as a consistent winner at bridge, bowling, baccarat, and roulette.

ONI did not seem to know, however, that in 1923 Yamamoto was excluded from the casino at Monte Carlo because of his excessive winning.[4]

But gambling did not occupy all of Yamamoto's active mind. He was fascinated by a book published in 1925 by a British naval authority, Hector C. Bywater, titled *The Great Pacific War.* In this prescient work, Bywater showed that Japan could create a nearly invulnerable empire by making a surprise attack on the U.S. Pacific Fleet, invading Guam and the Philippines and fortifying its mandate islands.

Bywater was born the same year as Yamamoto, and as a journalist, spy, and naval researcher, was steeped in the lore of unannounced attack and Japanese expansionism. He knew that James Gordon Bennett, editor of the *New York Herald,* had been predicting war with Japan since 1897, and that Homer Lea's 1904 book *The Valor of Ignorance,* which detailed a future American-Japanese war, had sold 40,000 copies in Japan alone.[5]

Bywater's first book on this theme, *Sea Power in the Pacific,* went through three printings in the United States in 1921 and was translated into Japanese and distributed to all ranking Japanese naval officers within sixty days of its American appearance. By 1922, it was required reading at the Imperial Naval Academy and the Japanese Naval War College, although forbidden to the Japanese public.[6]

Bywater's premise was that a direct assault upon Japan by U.S. forces was forbidden by distance (and its secondary fuel and supply consumption) and that the key to American success would be an island-hopping campaign through the Marianas, to Guam, and to the Philippines.

Bywater's occasional columns in the *Baltimore Sun* were widely read, and his subjects included criticism of the United States' decision not to fortify Guam (1921), the irresistible need of the Japanese to seize the Dutch East Indies (1923), and the British decision to fortify Singapore against the Japanese (1924).

In 1925, Bywater's magnum opus, *The Great Pacific War,* was reviewed in every major newspaper in the United States, Great Britain, and Japan. In this work, his final analysis of Pacific strategy, the war begins with the destruction of the U.S. Fleet by the Japanese and ends with a U.S. victory, won by advances via Hawaii, Samoa, Truk, Ponape, Yap, and the Philippines. Yamamoto studied Bywater's work when he was stationed in Washington, D.C. (After the war, Mitsuo Fuchida, who led the attack at Pearl Harbor, declared that he had read both of Bywater's books and that they were influential in "our study of the strategy.")[7]

It should not be implied that Bywater was the sole proponent of "island hopping" in a war with Japan. Earl "Pete" Ellis, a U.S. Marine

Corps officer, had proposed the concept in 1913, as had John A. Lejeune, a future U.S. Marine Corps commandant, in 1914. The following year, William V. Pratt, future chief of naval operations, and Alfred P. Niblack, future director of the Office of Naval Intelligence, gave speeches advocating an island-hopping strategy in any war with Japan. All realized the futility of steaming straight from Hawaii to Japan without resupply or air superiority.[8] In a final stroke of prescience, Bywater, writing in *Pacific Affairs* in 1935, predicted that the initial Japanese attack would be launched from aircraft carriers.[9]

Another aspect of Yamamoto's strategic thinking was his preoccupation with oil. Even though many ships still burned coal in the 1920s, he saw oil as the fuel of the future. Perhaps this was because he was raised in Niigata, Japan's only oil-producing province. In 1920, with funds out of his own pocket, he visited the oil fields of Texas and Mexico and marveled at the volume and low cost of the oil produced there. The Mexicans even made intelligence inquiries about this small, intense, note-taking Japanese man who, though a government-sponsored student, traveled in complete poverty.

Upon Yamamoto's return to Japan in 1928, he requested and received command of the new aircraft carrier *Akagi*. For the next six years, he devoted himself to solving the practical problems generated by the new theories of war in the air. His memoranda at that time showed his belief that naval aviation must rest on proper use of instruments and long-distance navigational aids, not just the intuition and seat-of-the-pants flying that had been the tradition thus far.

In 1934, during a trip to London, Yamamoto arranged to meet Hector Bywater. They spent a whole evening together in Yamamoto's suite at Grosvenor House, discussing Bywater's books and their implications for Pacific strategy and tactics.

From 1934 to 1939, Yamamoto served in top posts in Tokyo, where he studied the battle plan devised by the Naval General Staff. Basically unchanged since 1907, the plan envisaged luring the American fleet out to somewhere near Japan and annihilating it in a traditional surface set piece engagement, with battleships firing at each other and cruisers and destroyers dashing about, performing their usual duties. The only action envisaged in the Hawaiian area was a submarine attack on the American fleet as it headed for the great battle. For more than thirty years, the Imperial Navy had been training for this Armageddon. Although Yamamoto regarded the plan as hopelessly obsolete, the power to set grand strategy was closely and jealously held by the Naval General Staff.

Even though Yamamoto was vice minister of the navy, he had little power to influence strategic thinking.

Yamamoto made good use of his administrative posts in 1936. He was head of the Aeronautics Department and used that post to promote the development of the Type 96 twin-engine bomber, known to American pilots as Betty. The Type 96 was as good as any medium bomber of that era, with its long, sleek lines, 2,200-mile range (greater than the B-17), and automatic pilot. The 1,048 that were built served Japan well. In a move that received violent opposition within Naval Command circles, Yamamoto opposed the construction of the superbattleships *Yamato* and *Musashi,* believing that Japan's resources would be better invested in building aircraft carriers.

But late in August 1939, at age 55, he was named commander in chief of the Combined Fleet, with a concurrent title of chief of naval aviation, and began a series of brilliant administrative end runs. Rather than either implement or openly oppose the strategic doctrines sent down from on high, he began training his fleet for the strategies that he envisioned, reversing the usual order of things. First, he requested permission to extend the battle area of the official plan to include the Marshall Islands. This seemed like a minor change and was accepted without question. Later, he pushed the boundary of the official plan eastward to include Hawaii; again, the Naval General Staff seemed not to notice the significance of this expansion.

The annual naval maneuvers of October 1939 intensified Yamamoto's belief in carriers and naval aviation. "Hits" scored by gunfire were open to debate, since live ammunition was not used, but torpedo "hits" could be established without doubt—the torpedoes had dummy heads and were set to run at a depth that would carry them under the largest ship, yet shallow enough that their track of bubbles was apparent. The twenty-seven torpedo planes of Lt. Comdr. Mitsuo Fuchida's unit placed twenty-seven torpedoes under the keel of Yamamoto's flagship, the *Nagato,* in spite of the battleship's violent evasive action, tracer gunfire, and use of searchlights to dazzle the pilots. With live torpedoes at combat depth, the *Nagato* would have been sunk many times over.

During the spring maneuvers of 1940, Yamamoto stressed the attack of carrier-based planes upon the ships of the "opposing" forces. Again, the "attacking" planes "sank" every battleship. Yamamoto remarked to his chief of staff, Shigeru Fukudome, "It makes me wonder if they couldn't get Pearl Harbor." When the maneuvers were over, Yamamoto kept the fleet on a wartime footing, instead of the usual procedure of returning to peacetime conditions, citing the events of Europe and Japan's new alliance with Germany and Italy. (He had strongly, but privately, opposed the entanglement with Hitler.) But Yamamoto's eyes were on the United States, not on Europe.

In a locked drawer in his flagship, the *Nagato,* was a 500-page mimeographed book, *The Habits, Strengths and Defenses of the American Fleet in the Hawaiian Area.* A network of spies in Honolulu kept the book up-to-date. Yamamoto knew that the Pacific Fleet was under orders to conduct "training and target practice," not to prepare for immediate action. A training program requires a regular schedule, with fixed time in port, such as every Sunday. The single narrow channel of Pearl Harbor assured that even with full alert, the fleet would require many hours to escape to sea.

Yamamoto was further encouraged by sixteen years of publicly known American exercises in attacking harbors. In January 1924, during a mock attack on the Panama Canal, carrier-launched torpedo planes "attacked" battleships at Colón, only to be criticized by the tradition-minded naval umpires for "low-level stunting."[10] In Fleet Problem VII, conducted in 1928, the carrier *Langley* launched planes that rained flour bombs on Pearl Harbor, to the surprise of the army and navy "defenders." The umpires ruled that Pearl Harbor was destroyed.[11] By the next year, the two huge new carriers *Lexington* and *Saratoga* had joined the fleet. The 1929 exercises assumed a threat to the Panama Canal, with a "black" force of sixty-three ships defending the canal. After a series of complex maneuvers, planes from the "blue" force's *Saratoga* "destroyed" the canal locks and airfields on the Pacific end of the Panama Canal, while a lone float plane from the *Aroostook* "destroyed" one of the Atlantic canal locks.[12]

When the *Saratoga* began launching her planes in the predawn darkness, one old line naval officer considered the exercise to be suicidal.[13] Other officers saw the implications more clearly. The commander in chief of the U.S. Fleet, Adm. H. A. Wiley, called the nighttime launching of eighty-three planes from the *Saratoga* "an epic in the history of aviation," while another admiral called this massive pioneer air strike "the most effectively executed naval operation in our history."[14]

A second plan to bomb Pearl Harbor was conceived and carried out by Adm. Frank A. Schofield, who in 1932 devised as the annual training exercise Fleet Problem XIV, a plan that called for aircraft carriers to approach Hawaii undetected and attack Pearl Harbor. To the surprise of most naval officers, the carriers (*Saratoga* and *Lexington*) were completely successful in their assignment. Their planes swooped down on Pearl Harbor at dawn on a Sunday, and "sank" the U.S. Fleet.[15] (It is doubtful that Admiral Schofield knew of a lecture given by Lt. Comdr. Riunosuki Kusaki, an instructor at Kasumigaura Air Base in 1928, in which he advocated a naval air attack on Pearl Harbor as a way of initiating a war with the United States. The lecture was open only to a select audience, and only thirty copies of the text were made.)[16] During further exercises in 1938, a third carrier-launched air strike "destroyed" Pearl Harbor.[17]

The outcome of these mock raids received considerable publicity at the time but soon seemed to be forgotten. But not by Isoroku Yamamoto. He was nearly sure that a Japanese attack on Pearl Harbor could succeed. Late in the 1930s, to test his theories, he found a location on the coast of Kyushu that was almost a twin of Pearl Harbor: Kagoshima Bay. Yamamoto moved his carriers near southern Kyushu and sent his planes skimming in over the ridges from the north, following the winding Iwasaki Valley to the shore, where they launched low-level bomb and torpedo attacks on dummy targets in the bay. The local farmers soon learned to ignore this display, which they dubbed the "navy's aerial circus." But neither the farmers nor the pilots, nor even the captains of the carriers, knew the real meaning of this circus. This Yamamoto had kept to himself, locked in his head, under his own code name of Operation Z, a tribute to the memory of Admiral Togo and the Z Signal at Tsushima strait.

Yet Yamamoto, a realist, not a dreamer, knew that his raid was only a theory. In reality, his carriers would have to cross the Pacific Ocean, liable to be spotted by submarines, merchant ships, or long-range planes from Wake Island, Midway Island, or even Pearl Harbor itself. He also knew that the Americans were improving the radar installations high up on the slopes of Oahu, based on the success of the British radar, which was detecting the approaching Luftwaffe. In addition, the U.S. Army had 125 planes for the defense of the Hawaiian area, and steel torpedo nets were on order to protect the fleet at anchor in Pearl Harbor. He also knew that much of Pearl Harbor was only 40 feet deep, and that torpedoes dropped from a plane tended to sink from 100 to 300 feet before assuming their assigned depth. A torpedo stuck in the mud of Pearl Harbor was of no use to the Japanese.

Furthermore, Yamamoto had not revealed his scheme to his superiors or to the Naval General Staff, who were still committed to the long-planned battleship encounter. There was no historic precedent for destroying an opposing main naval battle force by aerial assault, especially in a shallow, defended harbor. Operation Z was perfect in theory—perfect when the only "enemy" were the rice farmers of Kagoshima, stooping over their paddies, not thousands of U.S. Army men, manning radar, antiaircraft guns, and fighter planes, defending a harbor too shallow for torpedoes.

How could he assure success, or persuade his superiors, when what he proposed had never been done before? This truly was something to worry about.

*Chapter Three*

➤

# The Formidable Stringbag

IN THE SUMMER OF 1940, THE BRITISH CLEARLY NEEDED TO NEUTRALIZE or destroy the Italian fleet at Taranto. A land invasion was out of the question; British forces were far too weak for any amphibious assault. A naval bombardment would necessitate approaching within ten or twenty miles of the coast, sure to arouse the entire Italian Navy, including their highly effective motor torpedo boats, as well as large numbers of torpedo planes and high-altitude bombers of the Regia Aeronautica (Royal Italian Air Force). The waters of Taranto were too shallow for submarine attack, and there were no British airfields close enough for a land-based assault by the RAF.

One option remained: an attack by carrier-based planes of the Royal Navy's Fleet Air Arm. For the task of assaulting dozens of armored warships, anchored in a ring of antiaircraft batteries, the Fleet Air Arm possessed adequate numbers of only one bomber type: the Fairey Swordfish, an enormous, robust biplane. The web of stainless steel bracing rods and struts that filled the space between the upper and lower wings gave these planes the nickname of Stringbags, for the net bags used by shoppers in 1920s England.

Its immediate predecessors were the Fairey Flycatcher fighter and the Fairey Gordon torpedo bomber. Then came the Swordfish, a design mongrel resulting from two different specifications by the Air Ministry and one from the Greek Naval Air Arm, which later lost interest. The result was a torpedo, spotter, reconnaissance, mine layer, and dive-bomber with either two or three seats. Remarkably, it was fairly good at many functions rather than being second-rate in all functions, which is often the case in a "compromise" aircraft.

After three initial engines were tried, the designers settled on the Pegasus 111M3 as the power source, turning a three-bladed metal propeller. The 690 horsepower engine drove the Swordfish at a maximum speed, in level flight, of 134 knots, with legendary reliability.

The heavy steel tube frame included strong points for catapult launching, aircraft carrier deck arresting gear, and a bomb rack, which could hold a 1,610-pound torpedo, three 500-pound bombs, or a long-range tank. In addition, a steel pyramid just in front of the pilot's face provided a strong point for hoisting. The wings were also steel tubing, covered with fabric, and were hinged to fold back for better below-deck storage.[1]

The pilot sat up in a circular open cockpit at the highest point of the fuselage, just aft of the wings. Behind him and lower was a large second cockpit with room for an observer and a gunner-radio operator, whose proper title was telegraphist air gunner (TAG). When a torpedo and a long-range tank were both carried, the tank was fitted in the observer's position, the TAG stayed home, and the observer did both men's jobs.[2]

At first glance, the Swordfish was obsolete before the war began. Of all the major powers, only the Italians still used biplanes as first-line weapons, and those were being phased out. The top speed of the Swordfish was only one third that of the Spitfire. At the battle of Cape Spartivento, Swordfish, burdened with torpedoes and extra fuel, were only forty knots faster than the Italian ships they pursued, which enabled the ships to outmaneuver them. Yet this slowness had its merits: easy control and extreme stability. Stall speed, the velocity at which the wings cease to provide lift, was only fifty-eight knots. In the search for the German battleship *Bismarck,* there were high seas and forty-five-knot winds. Teams of men hanging their weight on the wings were needed to keep the Swordfish from being blown overboard after their deck tethers were loosened. Each takeoff was timed so that the plane ran forward as the ship's bows dropped, and took off as the bows lifted; mistiming would send the plane straight into the next wave. The take-offs were successful.

These characteristics of slow stability were even more valuable in landing. On a dark night, with a wild sea, only the dim lights outlining the landing area would be visible, and these glowing spots and the deck to which they were attached would be pitching up and down the height of a house. Too low, and the plane would smash into the steel stern; too high and the plane would miss the arresting wires and be caught in the hydraulically operated emergency barrier. The low landing speed (about seventy knots) meant that if the ship were steaming twenty knots into a twenty-knot headwind, the speed of the plane relative to the deck was only thirty knots, consistent with successful landing under the most dreadful conditions.

A Swordfish normally approached to land at seventy knots in a three-point, tail-down landing attitude, held in the air by the engine. On passing over the round-down (stern), the pilot would close the throttle. The aircraft would almost immediately stall and bump onto the deck, the trailing hook catching a wire, which would bring the craft to a halt.

After some initial problems during development, the final version, the TSR11, emerged, a plane so free of vice that it was never used in training new pilots, since it induced overconfidence. It was hard to stall, and when it did stall, it recovered smoothly. It took off in a short distance and landed at slow speed.

The ability to fly slowly had its uses in combat. One Fleet Air Arm pilot in the Norwegian campaign was attacked twenty-six times by Messerschmitt fighter planes. The British pilot and his observer used the technique of making a steep turn at sea level toward the attacking plane, just as the attacker came into range. The German's high closing speed and the smaller turning circle of the Swordfish allowed the British biplane to escape the attacks with only a single bullet hole through the wing fabric. Most planes will stop flying if power is cut while entering a turn, but not the Swordfish. Using this maneuver over the island of Rhodes, another pilot evaded two Italian CR-42 fighters, one of which fell into the sea attempting to imitate the Stringbag's action.[3]

This sort of maneuvering is not to be confused with dogfighting, which is the attempt by two high-speed aircraft to shoot each other down. These slow Swordfish maneuvers were purely defensive; only the incautious pursuer was harmed. Sometimes, in addition to this tight turn, the gunner would fire tracer and the observer would fire flares (Verey's Lights), which some Italian pilots thought to be "Churchill's Secret Weapon."

Sturdiness, too, marked the Swordfish. Many returned with large portions of wing and fuselage shot away. Even the Pegasus engine seemed extra durable. In the torpedo attack on the German battle cruiser *Scharnhorst*, German flak shot the top two cylinders off the Pegasus engine of a Swordfish. The propeller continued to turn for two more minutes.

In a night attack on July 20, 1940, on the Italian-held harbor at Tobruk in northern Africa, six Swordfish flew in low over the harbor boom, hugging the water to avoid antiaircraft fire. One pilot struck the boom, tearing off his port wheel. He was able to maintain control, completing his torpedo run (sinking a large tanker) and returning to his base at Sidi Barrâni, where he landed successfully on one wheel at 5:00 in the morning.

A description of a practice dive-bombing run will serve to further illustrate the qualities of the Swordfish that endeared her to pilots. To begin the dive-bomb, the pilot peels off and stands the plane on her nose. All 9,000 pounds, 11,000 with bombs, begin to accelerate— straight down. The whistle of the wind in the rods and struts rises to a shriek. The pilot opens his mouth to equalize the pressure in his inner ears. The air-speed indicator climbs to 200 knots; the altimeter winds backward at a furious rate: 10,000, 9,000, 8,000, 7,000. But unlike most planes, the Swordfish maneuvers as smoothly and as docilely in a vertical plane as in a horizontal one. And even in the absence of dive brakes, the Stringbag, with its wheels and struts and other protuberances all slowing the descent, refuses to speed out of control. The plane does not disintegrate, but flies straight down until the pilot is almost into the water when, with back pressure on the stick, the plane levels and is soon moving over the waves. Even pulled out at an apparently suicidal 200 feet above the water, the Swordfish, well behaved and reliable, delivers its crew back to the horizontal world intact.[4]

A torpedo attack has all of the elements of the dive, plus a few hair-raising additions. First, the pilot, having spotted his target, pushes the stick forward and is dragged earthward at a forty-five-degree angle by his engine and by the 1,600-pound torpedo between his wheels. He begins the familiar screaming descent—turbocharger whining, bracing rods shrieking, motor roaring, the whole assembly vibrating. The airplane's natural tendency is to come out of the dive, but the pilot holds her nose down as the sea and the ships upon it grow ever larger.

At 500 feet above the water, the sea seeming perilously close, the pilot relaxes his pressure upon the stick, then pulls harder and harder, sometimes adding trim control, as the flight path levels. Now, 50 feet above the water, the Swordfish is rushing over the waves at 130 knots, with the most difficult moments still ahead. Just over the top of the engine, the pilot sees the silhouette of a ship that grows larger every instant. The length of the ship twinkles and sparkles as dozens of rapid-fire guns open up. Every third bullet is a tracer, its jacket burning with hot colored flame, fairy lights of death, seeming to move slowly as they leave the ship, zipping past the wings as their real velocity becomes apparent, two invisible bullets for every steel firefly. Meanwhile, the pilot has throttled back, slowing the plane, edging her into true and level flight, ignoring the crisscross of tracer, every thought devoted to the needs of the torpedo, now ready for release. The delicate gyroscope inside that metal fish does not take kindly to rough handling; launched wrongly, the torpedo will dive for the bottom or circle wildly or refuse to function at all.

In the final seconds, while near misses make fountains of spray around the wheels of the Swordfish, the pilot jabs the release button and the plane leaps up, free of its burden. Now the pilot pushes the throttle lever full forward, pulls into a violent climbing turn, and heads away from the target, jinking and twisting to avoid the still-flying tracer bullets. The observer stands up in his cockpit, secured by his G-string, leaning this way and that, looking back over the tail at the thin, white line of bubbles to see if it meets the side of the ship, which only moments before had loomed ahead in the pilot's sights.

War is never Christian nor sporting, and the observer's prayer is that the torpedo will hit home. He hopes that the ship that was trying to kill him a moment before will now disappear and that the war will be a step closer to completion.

When stationed in the Western Desert, 824 Squadron foreshadowed at Bomba Bay the brilliant possibilities of large-scale torpedo attack: Three Swordfish sank four Italian warships in less than two minutes. Hesitant to admit that three elderly biplanes had caused such havoc, the Italian radio attributed the losses to an overwhelming coordinated attack by torpedo bombers and motor torpedo boats.

Stringbags of 830 Squadron, based on the bomb-ravaged island of Malta, aided British troops fighting Rommel's Afrika Korps by sinking shipping bound from Italy to Libya. During a six-month period in 1941, Swordfish from Malta sank 110,000 tons of shipping and damaged 130,000 tons. Joined later by Albacores, they sank a total of 400,000 tons of Italian ships, an astonishing feat for "obsolete" fabric-covered biplanes. The RAF, rarely known to lavish praise on a sister service, stated through its Mediterranean Air Officer: "At night, we used the Swordfish for attacks on shipping. As a torpedo carrier, the Swordfish is superb. On more than one occasion, the Swordfish have destroyed entire convoys on their way to Tripoli."

In March 1941, the *Eagle* was ordered to support the British troops fighting the Italians in Somalia, but the Suez Canal was closed by Axis mines dropped from airplanes. The Swordfish, with spare propellers, spare tires, and other equipment lashed under their fuselages, flew across the desert, through Egypt and the Sudan and finally to the Red Sea without losing a plane. There they found the Italian destroyer fleet. Midshipman Sergeant dropped five bombs into the *Nazario Sauro,* blowing her to pieces. Sublieutenant Suthers dive-bombed the *Danieli Manin,* sinking her. The *Pantera* and *Tigre* were run ashore by their crews after being badly damaged.

By now, the *Eagle* had made it through the Canal, reembarked her planes, sailed round the Cape of Good Hope, and began the search for two supply ships supporting the German U-boats in the South Atlantic. Swordfish found the *Elbe* and dive-bombed her until she sank. The *Lothengren* surrendered to the plane that found her (a historic first).

In the sinking of the the *Bismarck,* Stringbags were crucial. HMS *Victorious,* not even in commission yet, was rushed to sea with 825 Squadron. In spite of some inexperienced crew, the ship not yet being worked up, foul weather pitching the deck thirty feet up and down, and an intense antiaircraft barrage raised by the *Bismarck* after she was found, the Swordfish put one torpedo into her side. It was not enough to stop her, however, and she escaped again into the mist.

A few days later, other Swordfish, from the *Ark Royal,* found the *Bismarck* again and put a torpedo into her stern, jamming the rudder full over. Turning in endless circles, unable to progress toward the safety of air cover from France, the *Bismarck* was finally destroyed by an overwhelming force of British cruisers and battleships.

Swordfish, though becoming increasingly "obsolete," continued to play an important role in Fleet Air Arm operations. Swordfish were among the many planes that attacked the *Tirpitz.* Swordfish from the *Hermes* helped suppress a German-inspired revolt in Persia. Swordfish from the refitted *Illustrious* sank submarines prowling near Vichy-held Madagascar and aided in the surrender of that huge island. Swordfish were present when the British left France at Dunkirk and when they returned at Normandy. Swordfish were part of the tragically unsuccessful attempt to stop the "Channel dash" of the *Scharnhorst, Gneisenau,* and *Prinz Eugen.*

By 1942, the Stringbag was being replaced as a front-line aircraft by Albacores, Barracudas, and Grumman Avengers, which left a new role for the Swordfish, with their superb short landing and takeoff capacities; they were ideal for the antisubmarine warfare conducted from the diminutive escort carriers.

Until the advent of these small carriers in 1941, the long-range German patrol planes, which guided U-boat wolf packs to the convoys, flew unmolested, far from the reach of any British fighter plane, except the occasional "disposable" Hurricane launched from a catapult and destined to ditch at sea.

The German aircraft crews were horrified and startled when Grumman Martlet (Wildcat) fighters, flown from the new escort carriers, suddenly appeared in midocean. More and more, the huge German Condor planes left their French bases, headed west, and never returned.

The escort carriers carried Swordfish along with the Martlets. In attacking surface U-boats, the Grumman fighters kept the German gun crews cleared from their decks, while the Swordfish arrived with rockets, bombs, and depth charges.

Crossing the Atlantic suddenly became safer. Before the escort carriers, U-boats were sinking forty ships a month. Soon, of twenty-seven convoys, only a total of twenty-four ships were lost. The U-boats, too, headed west from France, and many were never seen again. Deprived of their Condor reconnaissance and attacked when they rose to charge their batteries, the U-boats had become the hunted, not the hunters.

The horrors of the Murmansk run, through the frozen seas north of Norway and harassed by German submarines and surface raiders, were somewhat lessened by the appearance of small carriers with Swordfish aboard. In these icy waters, the remarkable Stringbags sank twelve U-boats and assisted escorts to sink six more. (Twelve were sunk by escort vessels alone, and one was sunk by a Catalina.)

To free the now fully accepted escort carriers for work in the East Indies against the Japanese, large, fast merchant ships such as tankers and grain ships (which do not need deck cranes) were given welded-on flight decks and a complement of four or five Swordfish and were sent off as "bargain basement" carriers, with grain or oil in the hold and warplanes up above.

Burdened with new appurtenances (such as radar and rocket gear) and new duties, the Stringbag flew on, but of all of her adventures, the night of Taranto might be said to be her finest hour.

The two principal torpedo planes in the Mediterranean in 1940 were the Swordfish and her Italian rival, the SM-79 Hunchback. The latter had a longer range, twice the speed, and three times as many engines, but it was the Swordfish, and the men who flew her, that changed history.

# Chapter Four

➤

# Platforms and Weapons

THE STRINGBAG, NO MATTER HOW FORMIDABLE, WAS USELESS WITHOUT a home, a nest in which to be replenished, to fly again. And once it flew, it needed a weapon, and in the torpedo it found a remarkable one, a silver tube barely two hand spans in diameter that could sink the greatest ships afloat in minutes.

The histories and origins of these two devices—the aircraft carrier and the torpedo—form a remarkable chapter in the technology of destruction.

Two factors will forever constrain the reach of a battleship: gravity and earth's curvature. From the moment a shell leaves a gun, gravity tugs at it, slowing the shell, pulling it ever downward. No matter how much gunpowder is crammed into the breech of a gun, it can never overcome the tendency for the missile to fall to earth, a tendency that limits gunfire to an absolute range of somewhere near thirty miles. As for visual guidance in pointing the gun, the tallest point of the highest mast in the clearest weather will enable a lookout to see about forty miles. Radar can extend the observer's gaze but cannot extend the limits of the gun.

On the other hand, a Swordfish airplane lumbering along at 100 knots could carry three 500-pound bombs for 260 miles, drop them, and return. This gawky skeleton of metal tubes, wrapped round with fabric, could deliver, for one tenth the cost, three times as many missiles as a battleship's gun, and more than eight times the distance.

A battleship has nine main guns; an aircraft carrier, even an old one, might carry thirty planes. A carrier salvo thus might consist of ninety bombs at a distance of 260 miles. Conceptualized in this way (an exercise beyond the ability of many admirals in 1940), the reach and punch of a carrier is a vast step beyond that of any dreadnought.

A third of a century before the Second World War, a remarkable man had visualized these inherent possibilities. Clement Ader, a French

29

inventor, wrote in his 1909 book, *L'Aviation Militaire,* that future navies would have aircraft-carrying ships. These as yet unbuilt ships would have flat decks, clear of obstacles; storage space for the planes would be in a lower deck. Aircraft would have folding wings and be raised to the flight deck on an elevator. Planes would land over the stern and take off over the bow. Some planes would always be kept in readiness, while others were being serviced or repaired (an ideal not always reached even today). Ader also predicted that the design of these aircraft carriers would include excellent nautical hulls, making them as fast as cruisers.

But in spite of the inherent power of aircraft carriers and their airplanes, three factors were at work to impede their development: the natural conservatism of bureaucracies, the frailness of the early aircraft, and the zeal of advocates for land-based, multiengine, high-level bombers, under a centralized command. Each of these factors operated in different ways in England, Japan, and Italy.

## BRITANNIA RULES THE WAVES

As Admiral Cunningham had recalled, England's earliest efforts to produce a carrier were marked by hesitant steps that bordered on low farce.

The thirty-knot cruiser *Furious* was modified in March 1917 and was given a 228-foot flight deck forward of the main superstructure. She could launch planes but could not recover them, so after its mission each plane either ditched at sea or attempted to fly to land. The maintenance plan apparently was that when the *Furious* ran out of planes, she would sail home and get some more.[1]

The senior flying officer, Squadron Comdr. E. H. Dunning, tried to solve the landing problem by flying parallel to the *Furious,* as far forward as the bridge, and then placing his airplane into a sideslip that would bring him directly in front of the bridge. He would then straighten out at the last moment and land. In his efforts to perfect this maneuver, his plane lurched overboard and he was drowned.

In November 1917, the Admiralty sent the *Furious* back to the shipyards, where a second deck was placed on the stern. Now there were two flight decks, one forward and one aft, with the ship's superstructure in between. A little runway connected the two flight decks. With the new arrangement, the pilots trying to land on the aft deck had to contend with the air turbulence produced by the midship superstructure, plus blasts of hot gases from the smokestacks. The result: Only three of thirteen landings were successful, and the new commander, Fred Rutland, was blown overboard and nearly drowned like his predecessor.

After the war was over, the Royal Navy rebuilt the *Furious,* eliminating all superstructures and finally evolving a totally flush deck. In this new, and at last practical, configuration, she served until 1944.

In the final rebuilding of the *Furious,* the forward end of the flight deck was terminated in a graceful yachtlike curve of doubtful utility. With no superstructure at all, exhaust from the boiler room fireboxes was led aft to discharge near the stern, an arrangement not used again because of overheating problems.

The early failure with the *Furious* inspired the Admiralty to build the first functional carrier. In 1916, the British purchased an unfinished 15,000-ton Italian liner, christened her the *Argus,* and installed a flush deck 550 feet long and 68 feet wide. There were two elevators to bring planes up from the hangar deck. The aft end of the flight deck was square across; the forward end tapered to a sharp point. Since there was no bridge, or island, the liner appeared much like a flatiron turned wrong side up. Equipped with the new Sopwith Cuckoo torpedo plane, she was ready for action when the Armistice intervened. During World War II, *Argus* was used as a deck landing training carrier.[2]

The Royal Navy's third venture into carrier construction was the *Eagle,* originally the battleship *Almirante Cochrane,* ordered by Chile and laid down in 1913. Construction was halted as the war approached and the ship lay dormant until 1918, when the Admiralty bought her and conversion to carrier began. With peace, this progress was slow, and she was not ready for sea service until 1924.

The problem of where to put the island, holding smokestacks, commander's area, mast, radio aerials, and lookout posts perplexed early designers. The first plans for the *Eagle* called for a bridge above the flight deck, spanning the full width of the deck, supported by very narrow structures on either side. The planes would land and take off under this bridge.

Fortunately, reflection on the wind turbulence problems, plus the possibilities of a plane ramming the captain's bridge, led to a final design with the island far to the starboard side, the pattern now universally followed. The *Eagle* was still functioning when she joined Cunningham's force in 1939.[3]

The next British flattop was the *Hermes,* launched in 1918. This ship displaced 13,000 tons and had a conventional island on the starboard side of her landing deck. *Hermes* was in the Indian Ocean in 1942, without her complement of planes—a dozen Swordfish—when the Japanese fleet arrived in that area. Fifty Vals and twenty Zeroes sent the *Hermes* to the bottom.[4]

The next carriers built in the British program were the sister ships *Courageous* and *Glorious,* both rebuilt from light battle cruisers in the late 1920s. Each displaced 23,000 tons and had a starboard island and a 730-foot flight deck. Their hangars could each hold up to forty-eight aircraft. The flight deck did not extend to the bow, but ended about 100 feet short, leaving a lower takeoff deck for fighters. Both ships had underwater Pugliese bulges, designed to withstand a 440-pound TNT torpedo head.

The first large British carrier to be laid down as such was the *Ark Royal,* begun in 1935 and completed in 1938. Overall length was 800 feet. The sides rose to join the flight deck, giving a more integrated, finished look than that seen in the carriers built by conversion. The *Ark Royal* could carry sixty aircraft, and when war arrived in 1940, she was one of the mainstays of the British fleet.[5]

One of the vulnerabilities of early carriers was the relatively thin deck. Any bomb penetrating this deck would explode in the hangar area just below, amid planes loaded with gasoline and munitions, producing instant disaster. But the weight of an armored flight deck, about 1,500 tons, would mean that a carrier would be very top-heavy. In ship design, to get one benefit, another must be sacrificed.

Thus the Illustrious-class carriers, laid down in 1937, had armored decks but had to reduce their airplane capacity from sixty to thirty-three, as well as eliminating the storage and crew areas that would have served the twenty-seven absent planes. Future events would show that the three-inch-thick steel decks, along with the extra fire-fighting equipment, enabled the *Illustrious, Victorious,* and *Formidable* to survive blows that would have destroyed a less-armored ship.

The Illustrious-class ships all displaced 23,000 tons, were 753 feet long overall, and could make thirty knots. The *Illustrious* and *Formidable* were completed in 1940, but because of a shortage of armor steel, the *Victorious* was not ready until May 1941.

## NIPPON WAIVES THE RULES

The Washington Naval Limitation Treaty of 1921-1922 set limits on all types of warships. The rules pertaining to aircraft carriers were based on total tonnage: a maximum of 135,000 tons each for the United States and the British Empire, 60,000 tons each for France and Italy, and 81,000 tons for Japan. No one carrier was to exceed 27,000 tons displacement or to carry a gun with bore in excess of eight inches. The treaty terminated in 1936, with provisions for renewal.

During this period, Japan was unhappy with its limitations and demanded parity with the United States and Britain. At the London Naval Conference of 1934, the last attempt to limit ships by treaty, Japan was represented by then Vice Admiral Yamamoto. He defended Japan's position with a dinner party quip, "I am shorter than you are, but I am not asked to eat only three fifths as much as my hosts."

When Japan's request was refused, the country announced in 1936 that it accepted no future limitations and would build as it pleased. Japan's future ship construction was to be not only unlimited, but also highly secretive.

It had not always been so. Between 1921 and 1923, the Semphill Mission, an advisory group of British naval aviators, helped train the first Japanese naval fliers and aided in designing Japan's first aircraft carrier, the *Hosho.* But as the 1920s wore on, Japan became less willing to trade technical information. Her naval architects worked in increasing isolation and secrecy to solve the complex problem of ever larger ships, without the background, experience, and wealth of data available to Western designers. With a smaller fleet and no iron or fuel resources, Japan strove for inherently superior ships, but without the technical expertise with which to balance the components of defense (armor), offense (guns and number of planes), and speed (narrow, light hulls). One cannot have all three. In spite of problems with stability and reliability, however, Japan did produce a formidable array of carriers between 1923 and 1940.

By 1936, Japan had passed Britain and caught up to the United States in carrier design. Their stress on offense, though, created some weaknesses. Their high-speed, lightweight carriers had room for many planes but neglected armor and fire-extinguishing capability.

The *Hosho,* a converted oil tanker, was completed in 1922. She displaced 7,500 tons and could make twenty-five knots. With a flush, 510-foot flight deck, she was able to accommodate twenty-six aircraft. The *Hosho* spent the years of World War II as a training ship.

Japan's next effort was the *Akagi,* a 30,000-ton carrier converted from a battle cruiser and first completed in 1927. In 1938, in her final form, she had an 817-foot flight deck.

The *Kaga,* also displacing 30,000 tons, began life in 1920 as a battleship but was converted to a carrier; after a 1935 refit, she emerged with an 815-foot flight deck, space for eighty-one airplanes, and a top speed of twenty-eight knots. She had the flush deck and absent island typical of Japanese carrier design.

The *Ryujo* was designed from the outset as a carrier, laid down in 1929 and completed in 1933. The profile was characteristic of Japanese design:

a very tall, boxy flat-topped hull, with a low yachtlike bow projecting well forward. This ship was small, only 8,000 tons. To make room for her forty aircraft, the architects put in two hangar decks, one above the other, producing a high, overloaded, and unstable ship whose bows were submerged by any large wave. A 1936 reconstruction strengthened the hull and raised the bow.

The *Soryu, Hiryu,* and *Zuiho,* all completed just as World War II began, continued the Japanese pattern of light armor and capacity for many planes.

The average speed of the British and Japanese carriers was identical—thirty knots—but the number of planes carried was much different: sixty-one per Japanese carrier versus forty-four per British ship. The British clearly chose armor over firepower. The wisdom of that decision would be judged by history.

Whereas the British hindered themselves by putting Fleet Air under land administration for twenty years, Japan's naval aviators enjoyed the advantage of a separate Naval Air Service, founded in 1912, just nine years after the first flight of the Wright brothers, and were more free to adapt planes and tactics to the actual needs of flying at sea. Yamamoto, who had learned to fly at Kasumigaura Naval Air Training Station, and his protégé, Minoru Genda, a brilliant pilot and administrator, set the examples of ambition and efficiency so necessary in forming an organization.

## A DAY LATE AND A LIRA SHORT

Italian naval aviation seemed off to a good start when, in 1909, Navy lieutenant Mario Calderara earned his pilot's license. In 1912, the Italian Navy had a flying school at Venice. By 1918, they had over 500 aircraft in naval service and a seaplane tender ship, the converted liner *Europa.* But already the advocates of a single, monopolistic, land-based air service, built around high-altitude bombing by giant bombers, were at work: Hugh Trenchard in England, Billy Mitchell in the United States, and Giulio Douhet in Italy. The latter's extreme views on aviation earned him a court-martial and a sentence of a year in prison; Mitchell, too, was court-martialed for his views.

In 1918, however, when Mussolini came to power, Douhet was recalled to service to head the Central Aeronautical Bureau. Five years later, Il Duce announced his plan to unify all Italian military aviation into one air force, the Regia Aeronautica. This enraged the navy minister, who resigned, and Mussolini, never overmodest, appointed himself as navy minister, in addition to his other duties.

In 1925, Mussolini decided that there was no need for Italy to have an aircraft carrier. In this decision, he was supported not only by the conservative admirals, but also by the generals of the Regia Aeronautica, who contended that Italy and Sicily formed one huge unsinkable aircraft carrier, eliminating the need for any ship with airplanes.

This all changed in March 1941, after the Battle of Cape Matapan, where the Italians lost three heavy cruisers and two destroyers, while the British lost just one airplane. Now Il Duce decreed that Italy would have an aircraft carrier—immediately!

The 38,000-ton liner *Roma* was to be converted into an aircraft carrier, to be christened the *Aquila* (Eagle). She would have new turbine engines to drive her through the water at thirty knots, would sprout eighty-two antiaircraft guns, and would carry fifty RE-2000 fighter-bombers.

A few days later, Italy's master leader decided that he needed not just one but two aircraft carriers. The liner *Augustus* was to become the carrier *Sparviero* (Sparrow).

But a country already short of funds, materials, and skilled labor does not build its first aircraft carrier overnight. Italy surrendered in September 1943 and neither aircraft carrier was ever completed. Even if Mussolini had built his carriers, the vast cost of maintaining them and the certainty that the British or the Americans would have sunk them suggest that he had been right not to build them in the first place.

## TORPEDOES

Aircraft carriers and their planes form two parts of a triad. The third element is the weapon, in this case, the torpedo. The planes that attacked Taranto dropped both bombs and torpedoes. It was the torpedoes that did the greatest damage. Part of the explanation lies in a statement attributed to an American admiral who was discussing the bomb versus torpedo issue: "In attacking a ship, it is more efficient to let water in from below than to let air in from above."

A bomb is a passive weapon whose own weight causes it to fall toward a target. Its path is determined by its position when released, the speed of the airplane from which it falls, and the density and movement of the air through which it passes.

A torpedo, by contrast, is active, not passive. A torpedo must be propelled; gravity does not draw it toward its target. Furthermore, it must adjust its course, both horizontally and vertically. If a torpedo strays to the left or right, it will miss its target. If it strays upward, it will hop along the surface like a playful porpoise, betraying its path and being deflected by wave crests. If it strays downward, it will pass far under its target or impact on the floor of the sea.

Added to these difficulties are the problems of both power and torque. A torpedo needs an engine that will run underwater, reliably, without access to outside air. The turning of its propellers develops an equal and opposite reaction in the torpedo, twisting it away from its initial course. This flaw also must be corrected.

The achievement of these complex requirements was accomplished remarkably early in its development, to an astonishing degree by a single man, British engineer Robert Whitehead.

Whitehead's first model was demonstrated in 1866, the year after the close of the American Civil War. Whitehead, who lived most of his life in the city of Fiume, Austria (now Rijeka, Croatia), interested the Austrian Navy in his device, sufficiently so that they funded much of his early work. His first effort, propelled by compressed air that drove an engine of his own devising, had only fixed fins to control both depth and direction. For this reason, Whitehead's first model tended to be quite inaccurate as to both depth and direction. To achieve a reliable hit, torpedo boat crews had to approach suicidally close to their targets.

For two years, Whitehead struggled with depth control. Then, in 1868, he conceived and quickly built a device in which the pressure of the water moved a flexible metal disc. Deeper water meant more pressure, which meant more disc deflection. This movement of the disc controlled the horizontal rudders. (The regulator in a scuba apparatus uses much the same principle.) Combined with a pendulum device to correct excessive oscillation, Whitehead's invention could hold a torpedo at a predetermined depth with an error of only six inches. He termed his depth-controlling invention "The Secret" and refused to patent it, believing that patent files were more easily stolen than the torpedo itself.

At this stage of development, the Royal Navy took an interest in torpedoes. In an 1870 demonstration before a board of three officers, Whitehead's device was aimed at the *Aigle,* a decommissioned wooden corvette. On impact, the torpedo blew a huge hole in the hull of the old ship, which promptly sank. The Royal Navy was impressed and entered into an agreement to build torpedoes, with Whitehead's permission, at the Royal Laboratory at Woolwich.

There, in 1872, a mechanic whose name was not recorded solved the torque problem by means of two propellers rotating in opposite directions, each canceling the torque of the other. A further refinement introduced at Woolwich was the replacement of Whitehead's vee-twin engine with a three-cylinder radial unit, manufactured by Peter Brotherhood.

By 1880, the Austrians were so impressed by the improved torpedoes that they paid Whitehead 20,000 pounds sterling (a considerable sum then) for the right to buy torpedoes from his Fiume factory.

In 1883, a complete set of plans was stolen from Whitehead's office. The culprit was never identified, but a year later, the German engineering firm of Schwartzkoff offered for sale a torpedo identical to Whitehead's. (The German director of this company had been a dinner guest of Whitehead's the night the plans were stolen.)

The Schwartzkoff firm, too, improved on the original design, adding a phosphor-bronze motor, that, unlike Whitehead's iron motor, would not rust. Since torpedoes are exposed, of necessity, to sea air and salt water, this rustproof motor greatly reduced maintenance.

By 1885, there was such enthusiasm for the new device that there was a worldwide "torpedo famine." Schwartzkoff was producing 600 torpedoes each year, and the Woolwich establishment 300, and there was still a backlog of orders.

Whitehead had become a wealthy man, but he still had not solved the problem of left–right deviation control, which sharply limited the range of torpedoes. Even a small error was quickly compounded when the range was 1,000 yards or more.

The answer came in 1895, in the form of a precision high-speed gyroscope, constructed by Ludwig Obry, which gave a directional reference point not dependent on external cues. The model first used in torpedoes had a two-pound steel flywheel, three inches in diameter, turning at 2,400 revolutions per minute. Linked to the vertical rudders by a mechanical amplifier (servo mechanism), the new gyro control reduced horizontal deviation to less than one half a degree.

The final step in the development of the Whitehead-derived torpedo was the heater, introduced in 1907. When a compressed gas expands, it cools. In an air-driven torpedo, when the compressed air leaves the high-pressure pipe system and enters the motor, there is a marked drop in temperature. Engines function better with hot gases than with cool ones. By introducing a heater, which warmed the compressed air before it entered the cylinders, the efficiency, range, and speed of torpedoes were greatly increased.[6]

From 1907 until the late 1930s, the standard torpedo in almost every navy had the mechanisms just described: Vertical error was controlled by the pressure-actuated diaphragm, horizontal error was corrected by the gyroscopic stabilizer, and torque was corrected by twin contra-rotating propellers. With the advent of the heater, this design reached its highest development.[7]

It was only eleven years after the Wright brothers' first flight that airplanes were used to drop torpedoes. The Royal Navy asked the Short aviation firm to build a seaplane powerful enough to lift off from the water carrying an 800-pound torpedo. There were several predecessors, but the Short 184 became the model that made history.

In August 1914, Royal Naval Air Service pilots, flying Short 184s and using 1897 model torpedoes, blew holes in three Turkish ships near the Dardanelles. A new era in naval warfare had begun.

With the Whitehead torpedo at its fullest development, a major new direction in design was needed for any one country to attain an advantage over its rivals. This advantage, unknown to the rest of the world, was created by Japan in 1928. Under the leadership of Rear Adm. Kaneji Kishimoto and Capt. Toshihide Asakuma at the Kure Torpedo Institute, the Japanese solved the problems of propelling a torpedo with pure oxygen. (Ordinary air is 80 percent nitrogen, a chemically inert element with no usable energy. With pure oxygen, however, 100 percent is available for energy production.) Oxygen gas is highly reactive; it eats away at most metals. The confined space in a torpedo means that the tubing and ducts must make sharp angles. The friction of the gas at these angles, as it bunches up and becomes turbulent, often leads to ruptured pipes and violent explosion. But persistent experimentation and engineering genius overcame these difficulties, and by 1933, the Shiki Sanso Gyorai Type-93 Long Lance torpedo was operational. The enormous advantage of this torpedo over its rivals can be seen in the table on the next page. By contrast, the American torpedoes in 1942, when fired at long range, were so slow that the Japanese ships could actually outrun them.[8]

In prewar maneuvers, it was absolutely necessary for the Japanese to recover every Long Lance practice torpedo launched, lest it fall into enemy hands. Sometimes the entire fleet combed miles of sea searching for a single lost torpedo. The Japanese efforts at secrecy were successful. In the spring of 1942, the allies were badly surprised not only by the range, size, speed, and power of the Long Lance, but also by the fact that it left no wake of bubbles as it raced toward its target. It struck fatally and invisibly.[9]

In shallow harbors, torpedoes tend to go deep and stick in the mud. J. D. Potter in *Admiral of the Pacific* states that the British at Taranto used wooden fins to prevent "porpoising." In reality, the Fleet Air Arm used a

## TORPEDOES IN SERVICE, LATE 1930s

### Airplane Launched

| | Diameter (inches) | Engine | Speed (knots) | Warhead (pounds) | Range (yards) |
|---|---|---|---|---|---|
| *British RNTF Mark IX* | 18 | B4H | 29 | 250 | 2,000 |
| *Japanese Type-94* | 21 | H | 45 | 867 | 4,900 |

### Ship and Submarine Launched

| | | | | | |
|---|---|---|---|---|---|
| *British RNTF Mark VIII* | 21 | BC | 40 | 750 | 7,000 |
| *Japanese Type-93* | 24 | OX | 49 | 1,100 | 25,000 |
| *U.S. Navy Mark 14* | 21 | TUR | 46 | 600 | 4,500 |

*Notes & abbreviations. RNTF: Royal Naval Torpedo Factory. B4H: Brotherhood four cylinder, heated. H: Heated. BC: Burner cycle. Type-93 is "Long Lance." OX: Oxygen. TUR: Turbine.*

fine wire cable, coiled on a drum, which connected plane and torpedo. When the torpedo was dropped, the carefully calculated length and breaking point of the wire placed the falling torpedo at the correct depth and angle.[10] The Japanese did not perfect a shallow-water torpedo until three months before Pearl Harbor. It used a breakaway wooden fin to stabilize running depth and direction.[11] Having solved the technical problem, they barely completed the Pearl Harbor torpedoes before the fleet put to sea.[12] Whether stabilized by wire or by wooden fins, the torpedoes of Taranto and Pearl Harbor made certain that any ship, unless surrounded by heavy steel netting, was a potential victim.

Airplane, carrier, and torpedo formed a deadly triad, one that was to dominate the seas throughout the war, with only the submarine as a serious rival.

*Chapter Five*

➤

# The Italian Navy
# and Air Force

## THE NAVY

THE NAVAL BASE AT TARANTO POSED A MAJOR STRATEGIC THREAT TO THE
British forces in Africa and afloat in the Mediterranean.

In the 1920s and 1930s, the Italians, with Pugliese as the leading design
engineer, created a series of warships unequaled in gracefulness and
speed. The Italian ingenuity in producing lightweight, high-powered
machinery and weight-saving hull designs was unrivaled. The cruiser
*Trento,* in 1929, maintained a speed of thirty-six knots during an eight-
hour full-power trial, astonishing for a ship that displaced more than
10,000 tons.

Italian design included not only speed and style, but also such innova-
tions as the Pugliese bulge, an ingenious underwater protective device.
The greatest menace to ships is the torpedo, which takes advantage of
the weight and incompressibility of water. A torpedo exploding against
the side of a ship creates a rapidly expanding sphere of superheated,
high-pressure gas. The weight of the water forms a cup, directing the
blast in the direction of the stricken ship, with powerful effect. Pugliese
designed a bulge in the hull running the length of the ship, below the
waterline. In the center of the bulge was a long cylinder of air, three feet
in diameter, surrounded by fuel tanks. Much of the energy of a torpedo
explosion would be consumed in crushing the long empty cylinder,
sparing the main armored hull, which lay inboard of the bulge. But the
Italian effort was not just in quality, but in quantity as well.

The Fascists under Mussolini came to power in 1922 and within a
few years had established a total dictatorship. Mussolini's wish to create
a colonial empire, dominate the Mediterranean, and impress the other

41

nations of Europe (in particular, France, Italy's principal rival in the control of North Africa), led Italy into a major ship-building program. Between 1923 and 1933, keels were laid down for eighteen cruisers, thirty-six destroyers, and forty-nine submarines. In 1933, the Italians redirected most of their naval construction to the modernization of two older battleships, and in 1934, to the construction of two new ones.

Two years before the outbreak of the Mediterranean War, Naples harbor was the site of one of the most remarkable naval demonstrations ever seen. Benito Mussolini, ever sensitive to a slight, felt himself over-shadowed by Hitler's annexation of Austria and invited him for a state visit.

A new railroad station was built expressly to receive Hitler in the proper style. The German leader, not to be outdone, arrived with five special trains crammed with Nazi party officials, military dignitaries, SS bodyguards, and reporters.

The next day, May 3, 1938, Hitler was taken on an almost surreal tour of Rome, laying wreaths at the Royal Tombs, the Tomb of the Unknown Soldier, and the Fascist Altar; lunching at the palace with King Victor Emmanuel; reviewing 50,000 Fascist youth on parade; attending a state dinner; and finally, listening to a serenade by 2,600 trumpeters, sounding the "Wedding March" from *Lohengrin*, Hitler's favorite opera. But all this was only prelude.

The next morning, a high-speed train carried the two dictators and their entourage to Naples harbor, where the king met them and joined them on board the battleship *Conte di Cavour*. Once aboard, Mussolini gave a signal, and all 190 Italian warships weighed anchor at once and sped to sea in perfect formation. In twenty-five minutes, the entire fleet had crossed the horizon and was gone.

At sea, the cruisers *Fiume* and *Zara* demonstrated their gunnery by destroying a target ship anchored eleven miles distant. As formations of planes flew overhead, eighty-five submarines charged toward the flagship, sub-merged simultaneously, and eight minutes later, surfaced, still in perfect formation, and fired a salute, eighty-five guns discharging simultaneously.

This dazzling display was exceeded only by an enormous electric sign spelling out "Heil Hitler," which emblazoned the night horizon over Naples as the fleet returned. Even Hitler was impressed. So were the dozens of naval observers from a score of nations.[1]

By the summer of 1940, the Italian Navy had two 13,000-ton cruisers, the *Trento* and *Trieste*, both equipped with eight-inch guns, and four 14,000-ton cruisers, the *Fiume*, *Gorizia*, *Pola*, and *Zara*, also equipped with eight-inch guns, with a maximum range of eighteen miles. The Trento class could do thirty-six knots and the Fiume class, thirty-four knots. In addition to these cruisers, twelve others were in service in the summer of 1940.

But larger and even more formidable than the cruisers were the six Italian battleships. Two of these were mint fresh, entering service in the summer of 1940, and four were older ships that had been completely rebuilt in 1939 and 1940.

The older ships were of two classes, Cavour and Doria. The Cavour-class ships were launched in 1911; when rebuilt in 1937, they could do twenty-seven knots, had newly installed Pugliese protective systems, and mounted twelve-inch main guns. When the war opened, the *Conte di Cavour* and her sister ship *Giulio Cesare* were both in service. (In 1934, Hector Bywater, in his role as a naval correspondent, was invited by Mussolini to inspect the Italian Navy. As a private joke, Bywater suggested that Mussolini modernize the *Conte di Cavour* and the *Giulio Cesare,* ships that Bywater regarded as utterly worthless. Later, Bywater was amused to see the millions of lire poured into these projects by Mussolini, whom Bywater privately regarded as a "strutting lunatic.")[2]

The Doria class comprised two ships: the *Andrea Doria* and *Caio Duilio,* both launched in 1913 and rebuilt in 1939. When refitted, they could do twenty-six knots despite steel armor ten inches thick. They both mounted main batteries of ten guns, each of which hurled shells thirteen inches in diameter. In addition, they carried secondary armaments of twelve five-inch guns, ten three-inch guns, and thirty-one antiaircraft guns.[3]

The two brand new battleships were the *Littorio* and her sister *Vittorio Veneto.* Fully loaded, they each displaced 45,000 tons, were 780 feet long, and had a crew of 1,800. Each ship had triple turrets, each mounted with three fifteen-inch guns. The steel armor alone weighed 14,000 tons and was eleven inches thick on the turrets. In addition to these formidable attributes, the *Littorio* and the *Vittorio Veneto* bristled with an additional sixty-two lesser guns. (When they built these ships, the Italians had no intention of operating outside the Mediterranean. When the remains of the Italian fleet surrendered in 1943, they were laid up in the Bitter Lakes of Suez as no use to the Allies, because of their short range.)[4]

Accompanying this flotilla of ponderous dreadnoughts were a large number of destroyers, high-speed "mosquito" boats, and torpedo boats, as well as the human torpedoes—tiny underwater craft, each with a human pilot in scuba gear sitting astride his explosive steed. With its modern fleet—an impressive array of ships to dominate the Mediterranean—and with many acts of courage demonstrated by Italian mariners, why was it that Italy did not win the war? Five major factors seem to have played a part.

First was the price paid to obtain the remarkable speeds of their modern ships. Narrow ships are faster, whereas wider, beamier ships are more stable. The cruisers and destroyers that raced through the blue Mediterranean waves could become rolling, pitching, heaving, yawing, shuddering demons in bad weather, catching great floods over their bows and leaving their crews wallowing in terror and seasickness. Further, the high speeds had been obtained in part by forcing the machinery, driving the engines and gear boxes to their limits, with the not surprising result that many of the ships needed frequent repair. The Fascist government initially had offered the shipyards a bonus of 1 million lire for each knot over design speed, but in the late 1930s the trend was reversed, and slightly slower but much more reliable designs began to appear.[5]

The second factor was the absence of an aircraft carrier, a decision made years earlier in the belief that the many land bases held by Italy were sufficient. In the eastern Mediterranean, the British had only the obsolete carrier *Eagle,* first laid down in 1913, but the Italians had none.

Third, if the navy wanted help from the air, it had to call upon the Regia. Combined operations call for cooperation and coordination, but interservice rivalries and jealousies blocked close liaison, rapid communication, and shared responsibilities. This was seen with powerful effect in July 1940, off Calabria, when, in spite of frantic signals from the Italian naval commanders, the Regia Aeronautica heavily and repeatedly attacked the Italian fleet. Count Ciano, Mussolini's son-in-law, wrote in his diary, "the battle was not a fight between British and Italians, but a dispute between our sailors and our aviators." On another occasion, British destroyers had stopped to rescue the survivors of the Italian cruiser *Bartolomeo Colleoni,* and the Italians mistakenly bombed their own sailors as they struggled, cursing, toward the British lifelines.[6]

A fourth factor, which aggravated the other problems, was Mussolini's proclivity for appointing high officers on the basis of political reliability and social connections rather than professional competence. These courtiers and favor seekers were more prone to jurisdictional wrangling than working for a common purpose.

The final factor was the concept of the "fleet in being," the notion that the presence of the fleet in and of itself, rather than its actual use in combat, is the wisest use of naval strength. Mussolini had ordered an offensive policy, but Adm. Domenico Cavagnari, chief of the Italian Naval Staff, believed that a defensive strategy was the best policy, to guard the home waters and the sea routes to Italy's colonies in northern

Africa. The unspoken message was that every commander was supposed to get his ship safely back to harbor and that sustaining damage was no route to promotion.

On April 9, 1940, Mussolini revealed his plan to enter the war with a sudden attack on the south of France. Adm. Cavagnari, who also held the post of undersecretary of state for the navy, sent Mussolini a lengthy memorandum in which he pointed out that Italy did not have the industrial strength to replace lost ships as fast as would the Allies, that Italy lacked reconnaissance aircraft of sufficient speed and range, that cooperative arrangements between the navy and the Regia Aeronautica were almost nonexistent, and that the naval bases lacked adequate antiaircraft defenses. Cavagnari concluded by saying that Italian losses would be heavy, and that by the end of any war, Italy would have lost its colonies, its navy, and its air force. No one could accuse Cavagnari of a lack of foresight.

The Italian Navy entered the war with several advantages. It had broken the British code and found that reading the enemy radio was often more useful than relying on the Regia Aeronautica's surveillance of the British fleet. In addition, the Italian Navy had a well-equipped operations room in Rome, the Super Marina, with telephone and teletype connections adequate for many simultaneous incoming and outgoing messages. But even with good intelligence, policy dictated caution.[7]

The British, on the other hand, recognized that losses were inevitable if wars were to be won, and that the intrepid, audacious, and aggressive captain was an asset, not a liability.

But bravery and aggressiveness count for naught if the tools to work with are limited. In July 1940, in the eastern Mediterranean, Admiral Cunningham had five battleships: the *Warspite, Barham, Ramillies, Royal Sovereign,* and *Malaya*. The *Malaya* had chronic condenser problems, preventing an adequate steam supply for reliable engine operation, and the *Barham's* guns could not shoot effectively at the ranges reached by the Italian battleships. Cunningham's seven cruisers had smaller guns with shorter ranges than those of the Italian cruisers, and of those seven British cruisers, the *Kent* had serious condenser problems. The battleships *Ramillies* and *Royal Sovereign* had failing boilers. The Egyptian dock and repair workers refused to work the day of an air raid or even the following day. At Suez, there were only 110 shells per cruiser, enough for a few minutes of active combat. With this ailing fleet were the *Eagle,* small and obsolete with an almost unarmored flight deck, 20 destroyers, and 12 submarines (Italy had 106), mostly outdated.

Whatever the administrative shortcomings of the Italian Navy, in June 1940, their British opponents were outgunned and outmanned by any measure of naval strength.

In addition to its modern ships and code-breaking capacity, the Italian Navy had a long tradition of professionalism and bravery, though this was often lost in Allied propaganda, which stressed Italian disasters and alleged lack of courage. In the Italian ships sunk, 30 percent of the enlisted men died, 50 percent of the officers, 75 percent of the ship's commanders, and 100 percent of the admirals. Clearly the officers did not abandon their men.[8]

In addition, certain specialized units were extraordinarily effective. The 10th Mas (motor torpedo boat unit), a highly secret group, launched hand-guided torpedoes ridden by frogmen. The extraordinary effectiveness of these units, which won the admiration of the British high command, enabled the Italians to sink British ships within the ports of Gibraltar and Alexandria, the two most closely guarded bases in the Mediterranean.

A factor that complicates assessment of Italian valor was its variability: On one encounter a sailor or airman might risk all, but on another occasion he might fail to press home the attack. In some raids, the Italians would drop their torpedoes five miles from the target; flights of bombers headed for the British fleet would jettison their bombs and turn for home when attacked by Fulmars. A possible explanation was that most Italians disliked the Nazis, felt that this was Mussolini's war and not theirs, and harbored warm feelings toward the British.

## THE AIR FORCE

Italian military aviation has a long history. In 1911, in a war with Turkey over territory now part of Libya, an Italian pilot dropped three grenades on enemy forces at Taguira oasis; this was only seven years after the Wright brothers' first flight.

In 1915, Caproni-32 bombers attacked Austro-Hungarian forces. In 1918, the Caproni-46 was scheduled for mass production by Fisher Body in Detroit; only the Armistice caused cancellation of this plan for American production of an Italian design.

There was a four-year hiatus in Italian plane production, but in 1922, following the Fascist seizure of power, Mussolini announced a major expansion of military aviation as part of his scheme for a New Roman Empire. In 1923, all military aviation was consolidated in the newly formed Regia Aeronautica, over the protests of the admirals, who wished a separate naval aviation service.

By 1928, the Regia Aeronautica had a Royal Aeronautical Academy, a school for airplane mechanics, and an institute for meteorologists. In 1931, specialized schools were established for fighter pilots, bomber pilots, and observers; the Regia was divided into four internal zones and three overseas commands: Sicily, Sardinia, and East Africa.

By the 1930s, Italian aviation had an international reputation for excellence. A Caproni biplane set an altitude record of 56,046 feet, which remains unbroken in its class. A Macchi-72 approached the speed of sound. In 1933, a group of twenty-four giant Savoia-Marcheti 55-X seaplanes flew from Orbetello, Italy, to Chicago (via Holland, Ireland, Iceland, and Labrador), astonishing the world. Italian aerobatic teams were acclaimed at air shows in a dozen nations.

As World War II approached, Italy had a considerable stable of combat aircraft. The most numerous of the fighter types were the fabric-covered Fiat CR-42 Falcon biplanes; almost 1,800 were built before the war was over. Although graceful and maneuverable, the armament of two small machine guns and a top speed of 244 knots placed the Falcon at a disadvantage in combat with Hurricanes and Spitfires. The Fiat G-50, an all-metal monoplane with retractable landing gear, was a step forward in performance but was still no match for British and German designs. Of 118 built during the war, 111 were destroyed.

In 1940, as the war opened, the Macchi MC-200 Arrow was the best fighter in the Italian stable, and more than 1,000 were built, but even the Arrows were thirty knots slower than the Spitfire. Nevertheless, in the Mediterranean that summer, this was of little consolation to the British, as no Hurricanes or Spitfires were available. Gloster Gladiator biplanes, and very few of those, were the only British fighters available to meet the Italian challenge.

Two bomber types formed the core of Italian heavy aviation: the Fiat BR-20 Stork and the Savoia-Marchetti SM-79 Hawk. The Storks were no match for modern opponents and were quickly relegated to raids over Albania, which had no air force. The SM-79 was another matter, however. Its three engines, one in each wing and one in the nose, drove it at 232 knots. The Hawk was developed from a sleek-looking transport; a gunner's cupola added behind the pilot position led the British to nickname it the Hunchback. Equally adept at high-level bombing and low-level torpedo dropping, the Hawk commanded respect.

Cunningham, eleven years later in his autobiography, gave the Hawk full marks. He described the efficiency of Italian reconnaissance and noted that the Italians seldom missed finding and reporting British ships at sea. Without fail, the SM-79 Hawks, each carrying 2,500 pounds of bombs, arrived within two hours. The usual attacks were made at altitudes of 12,000 feet, keeping in tight formation even under heavy antiaircraft fire. The bombers were unusually precise, considering the notorious inaccuracy of high-altitude bombing, as hitting a twisting, turning ship from a height of two and a half miles is very difficult. Cunningham recalled that on July 12, 1940, en route to Alexandria, twenty-four heavy bombs struck the water just to port, while twelve more hit the water near the starboard bow of his flagship. The nearby *Sydney* disappeared completely in a line of towering spray that reached the heights of the mast tops. Four days before, the Regia had scored a direct hit on the bridge of the *Gloucester,* killing Capt. F. R. Garside and seventeen others, and destroying the forward steering station.

Even though direct hits were rare, the frequent near misses not only were demoralizing to the British crews but also loosened fittings, pipes, and wires deep in the ships and threw drive shafts and steering mechanisms out of alignment. Cunningham was explicit that the Italian high-level bombing was the best in the world at that time and far more accurate than that of the Luftwaffe.[9]

Reconnaissance was a major concern of the Italians. In 1940, warfare was almost entirely visual. Long-range search craft were the eyes of every navy. For this purpose, the Regia employed two planes: the Cant Z-501 Seagull and the Cant Z-506 Heron. The Seagull had set a distance record and was steady and reliable, but she looked like a child's idea of a seaplane: High above the forty-six-foot-long hull was a single broad wing mounted far up on a tangle of wires and pylons; in the middle of the wing was a single nacelle, with the engine facing forward. Just behind the engine sat a gunner in a glassed-in cabin. The combat survivability of the plane was reflected in her nickname: Mamaiuto (Mama, help me!).[10]

The Heron was a three-engine monoplane with twin floats and could carry either bombs or torpedoes. With the latter, the Heron could be especially deadly. Attacking out of the setting sun or at dusk, the Herons were nearly invisible as they skimmed the water. When the British acquired radar in mid-1940, however, both the Seagulls and the Herons usually were shot down long before they could spot the British fleet.

In the Ethiopian war of 1935, the Spanish Civil War of 1936, and the Albanian war of 1939, the Regia was triumphant. But Italian aviation, so vigorous in the 1930s, became vulnerable by 1940. In brief, the early successes bred later failure.

Closer scrutiny reveals the reasons. The Ethiopian Air Force was equipped with a handful of antique Fokker and Potez biplanes, flown by a few French and German volunteers, as well as two long-forgotten black American heroes, John Robinson of Chicago and Hubert E. Julian of Harlem. But bravery was not enough, and the Italians controlled the skies. At the battle of Amba Aradam, the Regia dropped 396 tons of explosive on Ethiopian tribesmen who had no antiaircraft guns.[11]

In Spain, flying in support of Franco's Fascist troops was the Italian Legionary Air Force, with three fighter groups, four bomber groups, and five mixed units. The Loyalists flew mostly obsolete French and Russians planes, no match for the Regia Aeronautica. Mussolini's 1939 invasion of Albania was completed in forty-eight hours. The tiny Albanian army had almost no aircraft, whereas the Italian invaders had 25,000 troops, supported by 384 planes.

The politicians and propagandists in Rome proclaimed these to be great victories and ignored the protests of the professional military men, who were aware that Italian aviation was based on mass production of obsolete planes. At the close of the Albanian campaign, war with modern opponents was only months away, and yet the Regia had already exhausted itself by giving its best planes to the Spaniards and losing many other craft in the snows of the Albanian mountains and in the remote sands of Ethiopia.

Nevertheless, in June 1940, when Italy declared war on Great Britain, the Regia Aeronautica still had 475 fighters and 674 bombers, sufficient number to cause deep concern, even if many of them were not first-line machines. During the daylight hours over the Mediterranean, the bombers of the Regia Aeronautica made life very difficult for the Royal Navy; when planes of the Fleet Air Arm approached Italian naval bases, swarms of fighters rose to defend the threatened facilities.[12]

The air attack on Taranto was planned for the hours of darkness. The Italians had begun to experiment with night interception to defend the industries of northern Italy, which were being struck by British night bombers. To this purpose, a group of Fiat CR-32s stationed at Turin were painted black and equipped with long exhaust cowls to suppress the exhaust glow. But at the great harbor of Taranto, far south of Turin, there were no night fighters. The British aviators that night would face many dangers, but interceptor planes were not one of them.[13]

In the summer and autumn of 1940, the hard-pressed British forces in the Mediterranean faced a large, modern Italian Navy, based in home waters, and an Italian Air Force that was overwhelmingly superior in numbers but about evenly matched in equipment. British optimism was tempered by the knowledge that their Italian foe must be taken very seriously indeed.

*Chapter Six*

➤

# Malta and the Dog Mange Cure

THE KEY TO THE CENTRAL MEDITERRANEAN, MALTA SITS ASTRIDE THE east-west sea lanes from Gibraltar to Suez and the north-south paths from Italy to Africa.

Its strategic importance had been comprehended at least once before, four centuries earlier, by Suleiman the Magnificent, who devoted the treasure and blood of his considerable domain to a siege of the Christian forces that held that island. Suleiman's humiliating defeat was well understood by the Turks to denote a high-water mark in Islamic expansion. If not for Malta, the Île de la Cité might well house the Great Mosque of Paris rather than Notre Dame.

Malta's crucial role as a harbor, fortress, air base, supply depot, and reconnaissance outpost was still recognized by the British government in the 1930s, but because Britain was spread too thin over a world empire and had been underfunded too long because of the pacifism and faintheartedness so roundly denounced by Winston Churchill, Malta was initially written off as indefensible.

But the shores of Fascist Sicily could be seen from Malta on a clear day, and Italian bomber bases were only minutes away from the British facilities on Malta. Britain decided that Malta must be fortified and held. Thus Malta came to play a crucial role in the assault upon Taranto.

In the summer of 1940, the Maltese fighter defenses against the Italian Air Force consisted of three Gloster Gladiator biplanes (later nicknamed Faith, Hope, and Charity) and six pilots. Since the Italian bombers, mostly SM-79s, attacked at altitudes of approximately 16,000 feet and were faster than the Gladiators that were supposed to catch them, the only hope for the British pilots was to get above the bombers and gain speed by diving. But if the British were to wait at 20,000 feet in the hope that the enemy might appear, the Gladiators would most likely be out of fuel before any targets presented themselves.

Early warning systems were very poor, so the pilots sat strapped in their seats, their planes on the runway, waiting for spotters or the primitive radar to report incoming enemy aircraft. The pilots would then take off and climb full out to 20,000 feet. With six pilots for the three planes, one group would man the planes in the morning, and the other group would take the afternoon watch. The long hours of waiting in the hot sun in full flying gear were exhausting and dehydrating, and the pilots developed hemorrhoids from prolonged sitting. Group Captain George Burges recalled that none of the pilots kept diaries at that time, as they did not expect to live long. The combat reports that were filed were afterthoughts and hardly accurate. Later in the year, a few Hurricanes arrived, but the situation continued quite desperate. In the well-known Battle of Britain, 17 percent of the British pilots were killed in action; in the 1940 Siege of Malta, the British lost 23 percent of their fliers.[1]

For months, almost daily raids killed civilians and soldiers alike; homes, docks, airfields, and shipping were all battered. While this desperate battle of defense raged in the skies over Malta, another chapter was opening: the reconnoitering of the Italian fleet, a vital first step in any offense. And the key to Italian naval operations in the central Mediterranean was Taranto. The distance in a straight line from Malta to Taranto is 360 miles. The practical distance in 1940 was much farther, as a straight line would take British pilots across Sicily and the toe of the Italian boot. An easterly course was more prudent.

As Admiral Cunningham began to ponder how to counter the Italian fleet, his reconnaissance consisted of a few huge, slow, flying boats. These Short Sunderlands were new; the first had flown in 1937. They were high-wing planes, powered by four Pegasus XXII 1,010-horsepower engines. The Sunderlands were not hard to spot; the wingspan was 112 feet, and the tail fins stood 32 feet above the keel. Cruising speed was 160 knots; the normal range was 1,780 miles. These ponderous giants could be heard approaching 20 miles away. In spite of their valiant efforts, and their nose and stern power turrets, the Sunderlands were badly shot up in their attempts to photograph Taranto.[2]

Enter Glenn Martin. He was first a partner of Wilbur and Orville Wright, but in 1917, he left to form his own aircraft company. His 1930s Martin bomber designs included the B-10, an all-metal monoplane with a huge "birdcage" turret in the nose, and the Type 167.[3]

The first Type 167 was rejected by the U.S. Army Air Corps, but the design was offered for export, and in January 1939, the French Air Force placed orders for the Glenn, as the French aviators later called the plane. Two hundred fifteen planes were delivered before the surrender to the Nazis. The Glenns performed well in the few weeks of resistance to the Nazi panzer onslaught.

Upon the collapse of France, production of the Type 167 continued, but the succeeding planes, still in their crates, were delivered to England, where they were assembled at the Burtonwood Repair Depot beginning in June 1940. A total of 225 were delivered and assembled; most were flown out to the Middle East. The plane was officially christened the Martin Maryland by the RAF, but Churchill always referred to it as the Glenn Martin (and highly praised the craft), while the RAF pilots, with the British penchant for bizarre nicknames, called it Bob Martin, after a well-known dog condition powder marketed by Dr. Robert Martin.

The Maryland Mark I had two Wright 950-horsepower engines, which gave it a top speed of 251 knots and a ceiling of 28,500 feet. The fuselage was riveted aluminum, forty-seven feet long. The plane held a crew of three: pilot, bombardier, and gunner. There were four fixed wing guns, firing forward, and upper and lower rear-facing gun positions. Range was just over 1,000 miles, with a full bomb load. The fuel tanks were in the wings, with no self-sealing features. A single bullet could ignite or drain a tank.

Many of the initial evaluations of the new Marylands were done by Flight Lt. E. A. "Titch" Whitely, who found that at certain altitudes, the bomber could outrun a Hawker Hurricane fighter plane. This remarkable speed and general ease of handling led him to give the plane a good report. Two weeks later, he was ordered to lead three of the new planes to Malta to form a reconnaissance group. A direct flight took them over Nazi-occupied France and Fascist-controlled Sardinia, but the speed of the Marylands carried them safely over enemy territory before their presence was even noticed. They crossed France at night and arrived over Sardinia at dawn, where they each exposed a whole roll of aerial film, which they presented to the British photo interpreters as a gift upon landing. In Malta, the three planes were formed into a unit, 431 Flight, on September 6, 1940.[4] By late summer of 1940, the flight crews of the three planes had established a base of operations at the Luqa Airfield in Malta and were making wide sorties out over the Mediterranean, as far north as Naples, watching the Italian fleet, which seemed to be mainly in port, especially at the vast naval base at Taranto.

Whitely had as his crew Pilot Officer P. S. Devine and Cpl. J. Shephard. The number two plane was crewed by Flying Officer J. H. T. Foxton, Pilot Officer A. Warburton, and Sgt. R. V. Gridley. The third plane was flown by Flight Sgt. J. Bibby, Sgt. F. Bastard, and Sgt. D. J. Moren.

Soon after arrival at their new base, Foxton and Bibby were laid low by the "Malta dog," an unpleasant gastroenteritis, leaving only one pilot for three planes. Whitely undertook to train two of the navigators, Warburton and Devine, as pilots. Each had flown Ansons but were far from skilled. The Marylands had one vice: In a crosswind, they tended to swing into the wind. Because these were combat planes, not training planes, there was no seat for an instructor, and since the skies were filled with Italian fighters, the student pilots needed someone along to man the guns in case of attack. Thus each of Warburton's and Devine's training flights treated a terrified crew of two to unintentional circular takeoffs and zigzag landings, including one that ended with a long piece of wire fence hanging from the tail wheel. But soon 431 Flight had five pilots available instead of only three.

The survival of Malta depended on convoys from Gibraltar, and the safety of the convoys depended on knowing where the Italian cruisers and battleships were. Only the Marylands could provide that information. These three planes were so precious that Admiral Cunningham addressed a personal communication to Whitely emphasizing that the planes must be preserved at all costs. This meant that they must always run and never fight. The Marylands frequently saw Italian planes that would have been easy prey for their four Browning wing guns, but except for one lapse, when Warburton shot down a Cant Z-506 (and was reprimanded for doing so), the Bob Martins were observers and not fighters. Their crews exposed hundreds of rolls of film but fired only a few shots.

It is remarkable that so many sorties were flown without the loss of a single Maryland, as the Italians maintained a fighter presence over Malta much of the time, trying to catch British pilots arriving or departing (on takeoff, planes are clumsy with heavy fuel; on return, the crew is tired).

The Marylands were equipped with F-42 aerial cameras for high-altitude work. When there was cloud cover, the planes dropped down and streaked at low altitude and high speed over the Italian harbors, while the navigator took oblique photos with Whitely's Contax or a Leica borrowed from the Marquis Scicluna.

The first photo mission from Malta was September 8, 1940, only two days after arrival. The flight yielded perfect pictures of the harbor at Tripoli in Italian-held Libya. Within a week, Taranto received the first of its Maryland visits.

Now the question was what to do with the hundreds of photos generated by these flights. The art of interpreting aerial photographs was still in its infancy in 1940, and there was no one on Malta sufficiently trained to make the best use of what the Marylands brought back. The Royal Air Force Middle East Command had set up a photo interpretation unit in Cairo, and each new batch of photos was flown from Malta to Cairo for study. But this still left the navy in Malta without an interpreter of its own.

In early September 1940, when the aircraft carrier *Illustrious* reached Alexandria, one of its officers, Lt. David Pollock, was given permission to drive to Cairo and take a five-day course in photo interpretation. A week later, the now-expert Pollock returned to the *Illustrious* with a stereoscope.[5]

The photographs obtained by the Marylands became increasingly valuable—and alarming. A sortie flown on October 27 showed that the main Italian fleet was now at Taranto: five battleships, three heavy cruisers, six light cruisers, and a large number of destroyers—enough to pose a serious threat to the British Navy in the eastern Mediterranean and to any convoys approaching Malta.

As the Bob Martin planes became more persistent in their shadowing of the Italian fleet, the Italians redoubled their efforts to shoot them down. The British tried many tactics, such as approaching Taranto from the north, since Malta lay to the south of Taranto. But with such approaches, when the pilot made his final photo run, which had to be absolutely straight and level in order to get good pictures, he was a perfect target for both fighter planes and antiaircraft fire. On November 2, Warburton and his crew were photographing Taranto when they were attacked by three Italian CR-42 fighters. A bullet entered the nose of the Maryland, barely missing Sergeant Bastard, smashed through the instrument panel, and struck Warburton in the chest, knocking him unconscious. He fell forward onto the controls, throwing the Maryland into a steep dive. Sergeant Bastard wrested away the controls and flew the plane level until the pilot regained consciousness. They completed the seven-hour round trip from Malta to Taranto and landed safely. Except for a large bruise on his ribs, Warburton was none the worse, and Sergeant Bastard was awarded the Distinguished Flying Medal.

Five days later, the same crew, flying again over Taranto, was attacked by seven MC-200s from the 372nd Squadriglia. Churchill's faith in his Glenn Martins was justified. Even with a top speed of 310 miles per hour, the Arrows simply could not catch the lone Maryland as it returned, untouched, to Malta with a fresh batch of photos.

Three days later, on the afternoon of November 10, another Maryland from Malta confirmed that the Italian fleet was still at Taranto. Both the Italian admirals and the pilots of 431 Flight knew that all this aerial activity was hardly random and that some momentous event was close at hand. And were it not for the Martin Marylands of Malta, the Royal Navy would have had no idea what awaited them in the great harbor of Taranto.

In the next two years, Malta would be bombed again and again, by both the Regia Aeronautica and the Luftwaffe, and a great amphibious invasion of the island would be barely averted, because of Axis commitments elsewhere, but the role of Malta in paralyzing Taranto was already fixed on November 10, 1940.

*Chapter Seven*

➤

# The Plan

THE HEART OF THE PLAN WAS SIMPLICITY ITSELF: TORPEDO THE ITALIAN fleet in its harbor at Taranto. As with many plans, however, the details were far from simple, and it is the details that mean the difference between success and failure.

There are three principal ways to launch a torpedo: from a ship, from a submarine, or from a plane. Taranto lies in the great bight of the Gulf of Taranto. Any ship approaching would be detected far at sea and attacked from the many airfields on the surrounding coast. A submarine would have to slip by the picket boats of the harbor approach channel, get through the nets at the entrance, and then surface in the middle of the harbor, only forty-five feet deep—far too shallow for any submarine. Airborne was the only feasible option.

The idea of an airborne torpedo attack at Taranto had its birth in 1935, when Italy was invading Abyssinia and boasting of Mare Nostrum (Our Ocean). The Nazi-Fascist flirtation that would culminate in the 1936 proclamation of the Rome-Berlin Axis was already well advanced. The German annexation of Czechoslovakia lay three years in the future, but it was not difficult to envision a shooting war on the blue waters of the Mediterranean.

Adm. Dudley Pound, who commanded the Mediterranean fleet in 1935, ordered the preparation of a plan for an air-launched torpedo attack on Taranto. This plan sat in a navy safe for three years, until 1938, when Capt. Arthur L. St. George Lyster arrived to take command of the *Glorious,* then the only British carrier in the Mediterranean.[1]

Lyster, ironically, was a cavalier of the Order of the Crown of Italy, for his World War I service at Taranto. Although he was a gunnery specialist, he foresaw the eclipse of the battleship and the ascendancy of the carrier, which could project its force for hundreds of miles. Lyster's arrival in the Mediterranean coincided with the Munich crisis, and Admiral Pound, concerned that Hitler might not be satisfied with the gift of Czechoslovakia, requested that Lyster review the plan made several years earlier, update it, and test its precepts. On board the *Glorious,* Lyster had one squadron of Osprey fighters and two squadrons of Swordfish. He set his pilots to work, and after months of intensive training in night attacks, rapid launch and recovery exercises, and air–sea coordination, Lyster and his senior officers decided that the plan was plausible, given surprise and luck. He conveyed his findings to Pound, and the revised plan went back into the safe.[2]

In the summer of 1940, Lyster, now Rear Admiral Aircraft Carriers Mediterranean (RAA Med), and many of his trained men were transferred to the newly arrived *Illustrious,* commanded by Capt. Denis W. Boyd. Comdr. "Streamline" Robertson was commander (flying). The *Glorious* sailed for Norway, where she was soon lost. In September 1940, Lyster presented the updated plan to Cunningham at a meeting at Alexandria.

By now, Britain's position was perilous. France had collapsed, its Navy sunk or in German hands. The British Army had lost its equipment at Dunkirk and had been driven from Norway. America showed no interest in entering the war. The Italians, who outnumbered the British defenders of Egypt almost ten to one, had advanced to Sidi Barrâni, less than a day's drive from Cairo, and at home the Blitz still raged, with London in flames. This was clearly not a time for the faint at heart.

Cunningham saw that amid all these difficulties, he possessed three strong cards: the morale of his men, Lyster's trained air crews, and the reliable photo data from the Marylands at Malta.

The Taranto plan was finalized under the name of Operation Judgment and was a portion of a larger plan, Operation MB8, which involved forces derived from three different centers: the British base at Gibraltar, the island of Malta, and the British facility at Alexandria, Egypt. The plan made use of existing forces and needs in a pattern that would bring needed reinforcements to Malta, add ships to Cunningham's eastern fleet, and create such confusion for Italian intelligence that Taranto might be approached without detection.

By mid-October, the crews of both the *Eagle* and the *Illustrious* had completed a series of rigorous exercises, including night flying, and were considered ready for the attack planned.

Additional British naval units were about to make the hazardous passage from Gibraltar to Alexandria. These reinforcements, which included one battleship, two cruisers, and three destroyers, carried not only their own crews, but also crammed into every available space men and supplies to be dropped off during a brief stop at Malta.

The complete plan involved four supply convoys and three groups made up entirely of naval craft. The first convoy was MW3, out of Alexandria, comprising five freighters bound for Malta and three, loaded with guns and ammunition, destined for Suda Bay on Crete. The second convoy, AN6, consisting of three ships loaded with gasoline, departed Egypt for Greece. The third convoy, ME3, contained four large, fast (capable of fifteen knots or more) freighters returning empty from Malta, bound for Alexandria. The fourth, AS5, was mainly empty freighters en route to Alexandria from Greece and Turkey.

The three naval groups were Adm. James Somerville's Force H out of Gibraltar, Admiral Cunningham's fleet based in Alexandria, and the reinforcements coming from Gibraltar to Alexandria, which consisted of the battleship *Barham,* the cruisers *Berwick* and *Glasgow,* and three destroyers.

In the original plan, after all the ships had safely converged on Malta, Force H would head back toward Gibraltar, while Cunningham's reinforced fleet would divide into three groups. The first, Force X, a small group of cruisers under Vice Admiral Pridham-Wippell, would enter the mouth of the Adriatic Sea and create a diversion by making a night attack on Italian shipping. The second, a carrier group with the *Eagle* and *Illustrious,* would make the actual attack upon Taranto. The third group, consisting of all the remaining naval ships, would rendezvous at a point west of Crete with the other two groups after the attack.

The carrier group would launch their planes at about 9:00 P.M. from a spot just west of the Greek island of Cephalonia, about 200 miles southeast of Taranto. Every Swordfish from both carriers, a total of thirty planes, would be used. The attack would be made in two waves, each about an hour apart. Two thirds of each wave would be armed with torpedoes, while the remaining third would carry bombs. Some of the bomb-equipped planes would also carry flares for illuminating the harbor.

The exact path of attack would be decided the evening of the raid by the squadron commanders, based on the most recent photo reconnaissance. In general, the torpedo-equipped planes would strike the battleships moored in the outer harbor (Mar Grande), while the bombers would strike ships and installations in the inner basin (Mar Piccolo). Two of the latter planes would drop magnesium parachute flares before making their bombing runs.

Aerial photos in late October had shown the large number of anti-aircraft guns around the harbor. The intelligence estimate was that half the Swordfish would be shot down during the attack. The pilots were not told of this estimate.

The attack date was set for the evening of October 21, 1940, the anniversary of the Battle of Trafalgar.[3]

# Chapter Eight

➤

# Murphy's Law
# and the Final Plan

MURPHY'S LAW STATES THAT IF SOMETHING CAN GO WRONG, IT WILL. AND it did. A few days before the attack planned for Trafalgar Day, the Swordfish planes aboard the *Illustrious* were being fitted with additional gas tanks to extend their range. This operation was taking place in the enclosed hangar deck. A fitter slipped and fell, and his screwdriver contacted two live electrical terminals in the airplane's cockpit. The spark ignited gasoline dripping from an auxiliary tank that had not been properly drained. In seconds, flames engulfed the first Swordfish and jumped to others nearby. Fire sprinklers came into action, drenching the area with seawater, and in a few minutes the inferno was under control, but two of the planes were totally destroyed, and five others were soaked in salt water and vital parts were already corroding. The damage, injuries, and confusion meant that the Taranto attack must be postponed.

A few days later, Italy invaded Greece. In addition to the burdens already on Cunningham's ships, they were now obliged to provide convoy cover to transports taking men and supplies to Crete and to the Greek mainland.

In early November, as a revised attack schedule was being finalized, it was discovered that the *Eagle* badly needed repairs. The many near misses during the July 11, 1940, bombing attack had jarred the complex system of pipes that conveyed aviation gasoline within the ship. The danger of fire or explosion was too great if left unmended. Now, instead of two aircraft carriers, there was only one. Five of *Eagle*'s Swordfish aircraft were transferred to the *Illustrious,* but the total striking force was reduced to twenty-four planes.

Then, during the daylight hours of November 9, the *Illustrious* launched a Swordfish on a routine patrol. A minute after takeoff, the engine stopped dead, and the plane made a forced landing in the water. The crew was rescued, but the plane sank. A few hours later, a second Swordfish also crashed after sudden engine failure. Again, the crew was rescued but the plane was lost. The following morning, a freshly launched Swordfish had climbed to 1,500 feet when its engine, too, cut out suddenly. Another crew was rescued, a third plane lost. Now twenty-one planes remained.

Comdr. (Flying), James Robertson noted that all three lost planes belonged to Number 819 squadron. He ordered the tanks of the remaining planes drained and inspected. All of the fuel tanks contained water and sand, as well as a funguslike growth on the tank baffles. All of the planes had been fueled from the same supply point. (Later investigation showed that the contaminated fuel had come from the tanker *Toneline.*) No more planes were fueled from that tank, and no more engines quit.

A few days earlier, the latest photos from the Malta reconnaissance had presented another problem. Although the weather had been excellent, all of the prints showed rows of little white blobs. Lieutenant Pollock had been flown from the *Illustrious,* moored at Alexandria, to Cairo to review the photos with the more senior experts. He and the RAF photo interpreter puzzled over the blobs for many long minutes. Then Pollock suggested that they were barrage balloons: tethered balloons on a few hundred feet of steel cable, set up in rows to shear the wings off unwary planes.

Pollock asked to show the photos to his people on the *Illustrious.* The RAF man was polite but firm: The photos were to stay in Cairo. Pollock, ever resourceful, waited until he was alone, pocketed the relevant photos, drove to the Cairo airport, and had his Swordfish pilot-chauffeur fly him the 100 miles to Alexandria, where he reviewed the pictures with Cunningham's chief of staff, Adm. Algernon Willis. After his talk with Willis, Pollock returned to the *Illustrious,* and while he slept, the *Illustrious's* photo lab copied the pictures. Early the next morning, Pollock flew back to Cairo and returned the unmissed photos to their folder. In due course, an official RAF opinion was delivered on the subject of barrage balloons, but the navy had already modified its plan to take them into account.

Although the Italians had nothing in the way of radar, the area around Taranto was guarded by thirteen huge electrical listening devices that could hear an airplane many miles away. There were three rows of barrage balloons: one along the eastern edge of the harbor, one on the mile-long Diga (breakwater) di Tarantola, and a third in the middle of the cruiser anchorage in the northern half of the main harbor. What the British could not have known, however, is that of ninety balloons recently installed, sixty had been destroyed in bad weather around November 6 and had not been replaced, because of a shortage of hydrogen.

Scattered around the periphery of the harbor were 21 batteries of four-inch antiaircraft guns, 84 automatic cannons of twenty and thirty-seven millimeters, and 109 light machine guns. Twenty-two modern searchlights were ready to illuminate attacking planes and dazzle the pilots, destroying their night vision.

The six battleships, seven cruisers, and twenty-eight destroyers in the inner and outer harbors of Taranto mounted more than 600 antiaircraft machine guns. Further, under the surface of the water were huge steel mesh nets that could catch torpedoes. These nets, suspended from buoys, extended across much of the harbor. The harbor authorities had ordered 14,000 yards of net, but several senior Italian officers feared that the nets would interfere with ship's maneuvering, so only 4,600 yards of netting were in position on November 11, 1940.

The admiral in charge of the port, Arturo Riccardi, was fully aware of the likelihood of an airborne torpedo attack, and at nightfall the harbor defenses were put on high alert. In an official report by the Italian commander in chief afloat to the chief of naval staff, dated November 10, 1940, he enumerated the guns, searchlights, listening devices, and nets and described the plans for dealing with moonlight attacks, the scheme for coordinating shore-based guns with those on ships, the clear anticipation of imminent attack, and the extensive state of readiness.[1]

In brief, twenty-one slow, heavily laden, canvas-covered airplanes were to launch an attack against battleships with armor ten inches thick, in a harbor with approximately 800 antiaircraft guns, against an enemy that was expecting them. The sky contained thirty steel cables suspended from balloons, and the sea held 12,000 linear feet of steel nets to catch torpedoes.

With the loss of the *Eagle*, several Swordfish, and a revised timetable, the final plan, glorious in its complexity, took the following form.

The naval craft were organized for this operation into six groups. Force A consisted of the battleships *Warspite*, *Malaya*, and *Valiant;* the aircraft carrier *Illustrious;* the cruisers *Gloucester* and *York;* and the destroyers *Hyperion*, *Havock*, *Hero*, *Hereward*, *Hasty*, *Ilex*, *Decoy*, *Defender*, *Nubian*, *Mohawk*, *Janus*, *Juno*, and *Jervis.*

Force B contained the cruisers *Ajax* and *Sydney.* Their initial assignment was to take troops and equipment from Port Said in Egypt to Suda Bay on the northern shore of Crete and there get Bofors antiaircraft guns mounted. The *Sydney* was then to join Force A; the *Ajax* was to remain at Suda Bay until relieved by the *Calcutta*, and then also join Force A. Force C consisted merely of the cruiser *Orion*, which was to take RAF supplies and personnel to Piraeus, the harbor near Athens, and then to proceed to Suda Bay. Force D, comprised the battleship *Ramillies;* the antiaircraft ships *Coventry* and *Calcutta;* the destroyers *Vampire*, *Voyager*, *Waterhen*, *Dainty*, *Diamond*, and *Wryneck;* the trawlers *Kingston Coral* and *Sindonis;* and the minesweeper *Abingdon*.

Force F consisted of reinforcements from England bound for the Mediterranean fleet: the battleship *Barham;* the cruisers *Berwick* and *Glasgow;* and the destroyers *Griffin*, *Greyhound*, and *Gallant*. Force F also contained, on temporary loan from Force H, the destroyers *Faulknor*, *Fortune*, and *Fury*.

Force H, based at Gibraltar under Vice Adm. Sir James Somerville, escorted Force F as far as Malta and returned to its Gibraltar base. For this operation, Force H consisted of the aircraft carrier *Ark Royal;* the cruiser *Sheffield;* and the destroyers *Duncan*, *Isis*, *Foxhound*, *Forester*, and *Firedrake*.

Intimately connected with these six naval forces were four convoy groups of supply and transport ships. Convoy AN6, carrying gasoline and bunker fuel from Egypt to Greece, sailed on November 4 from Port Said and consisted of the Dutch ship *Abinda* and the British ships *Pass of Balmaha* and *British Sergeant*. The convoy was limited to seven knots because the armed trawlers *Kingston Coral* and *Sindonis* were even slower than the merchant ships. This convoy was escorted part of the way by the antiaircraft ship *Calcutta*. As they neared Crete, the *Calcutta* went ahead to assist operations at Suda Bay, which was still quite undeveloped, and the convoy steamed on along the northern coast of Crete, arriving safely in Piraeus with its anxiously awaited cargo of supplies and gasoline. To its good fortune, it had seen nothing of enemy submarines or aircraft.

Convoy MW3, which left Alexandria, Egypt, on November 5, consisted of the transports *Waiwera*, *Devis*, *Plumleaf*, *Volo*, and *Rodi*, bound for Malta, and two ships headed for Suda Bay: the *Brisbane Star*, carrying trucks and mobile antiaircraft guns, and the *Brambleleaf*, with bunker fuel and gasoline. On November 8, MW3 rendezvoused with Force A halfway between Crete and Malta, and the naval vessels took a covering position to the north of the convoy. Near noon that day, an Italian reconnaissance craft spotted the convoy and radioed its position before being chased off by Gladiators. At this point, the fleet and the convoy were about 180 miles from Sicily. Before 2:00 P.M., seven SM79 bombers appeared; British Fulmars shot down two, and the remaining five bombers dropped their bombs at random and returned to Sicily. The following day, the *Ramillies* and three destroyers were detached to convoy MW3 to its destination on Malta, while the remainder of the fleet remained at sea. Italian reconnaissance craft continued to shadow the fleet, and one was shot down. Convoy MW3 arrived safely at Malta.

Convoy ME3 consisted of four large, empty ships of fast transport design (fifteen knots), the *Memnon, Lanarkshire, Clan Macaulay,* and *Clan Ferguson,* escorted by the *Ramillies, Coventry, Decoy,* and *Defender.* This group proceeded without incident to Alexandria, arriving on November 13. The convoy was probably attacked that night by an Italian submarine, because three explosions were felt, although no ship was actually hit. Italian radio reported a successful attack by a submarine, but most likely the torpedoes had gone astray and struck the bottom of the ocean.

Convoy AS5, made up of empty freighters, proceeded without incident from Greece and Turkey to Alexandria.

Following the successful landing of the convoys, the Gibraltar-based ships turned west toward their home port, and the Mediterranean fleet turned its attention to the two remaining tasks: the air attack on Taranto and a secondary, to some extent diversionary, attack on nighttime Italian shipping between southern Italy and Albania. This diversionary raid was to be carried out by a force (temporarily termed Force X) consisting of the cruisers *Orion, Sydney,* and *Ajax,* with the destroyers *Nubian* and *Mohawk,* under the command of Vice Admiral Pridham-Wippell.[1]

The carrier force under Rear Admiral Lyster in the *Illustrious,* accompanied by four cruisers (the *Gloucester, Berwick, Glasgow,* and *York*) and four destroyers, departed from its position halfway between Crete and Malta and headed north as darkness fell.[2]

In spite of the plan's complexity, all ships arrived as scheduled, and because of its complexity, the Italians were deeply confused.

## Chapter Nine

> ➤

# Judgment Night

THE MINUET OF SHIPS ACROSS THE MEDITERRANEAN IN THE FIRST TEN days of November 1940 was mind-boggling, even in hindsight. The entire set of movements involved in Operation MB8 included Somerville's force from Gibraltar, Cunningham's force from Alexandria, and the new additions, which were attached to Somerville until they reached Malta, as well as four convoys of freighters. Involved in the operation were a total of five battleships, two aircraft carriers, ten cruisers, thirty destroyers, three trawlers, and innumerable merchant ships. The portion of this activity directly involved in the Taranto attack was called Operation Judgment and included the *Illustrious,* four cruisers, and several destoyers.

The Italian Operations Room in Rome, the Supermarina, tried to keep track of every ship but became increasingly confused, not only because of the numbers and changing composition of the groups, but also because their reconnaissance planes were disappearing instead of providing needed information.

With radar-guided intercepts possible, it was the British planes, not the Italian ones, that produced nasty surprises, quite the opposite from events a few months before. A three-day diary makes the point: On November 8, the *Illustrious* dispatched two fighters, which shot down a Cant Z-501 of 186th Squadriglia, piloted by Tenente Paolo Primatesta. Three of the Italian crew survived the crash landing and climbed into a rubber raft, which began to deflate. Despite a rough sea, a British flying boat landed and rescued them. Later the same day, the radar of the *Illustrious* detected the approach of fifteen SM-79 bombers. Three Fulmar fighters intercepted them and drove them off. None reached the British fleet.

On November 9, a Cant Z-506 plane from the 170th Squadriglia, searching for the British fleet, was attacked by a Fulmar. The seaplane, piloted by Sottotenente Tealdo Euria, dodged through the clouds trying without success to escape its pursuer. Euria and his crew were lost.

The next day, a Cant Z-501 of the 144th Squadriglia, based at Stagnone, piloted by Sottotenente Alfio Ferri, fell from the sky at noon. An hour later, nine SM-79 bombers, headed toward the British fleet, were driven off by Fulmars, once again vectored by radar to intercept the Italians long before they could reach their destination. One SM-79 fell into the sea.[1]

Comdr. Marc' Antonio Bragadin, chief of the Operations Intelligence Section in the Supermarina on the night of November 11-12, 1940, said that the reports coming in were so confusing and contradictory that it was only years after the war, when British records became available to him, that he was able to understand the events that unfolded that night on the dark waters of the Mediterranean.[2]

In the late afternoon of November 10, the *Illustrious* and her escorts had left Force A and steamed to the northeast, headed for a point just off the west coast of the island of Cephalonia in the Ionian Sea. There, just before 9:00 P.M. on November 11, the first wave of Swordfish lifted off the deck of the *Illustrious* and headed toward Taranto.

The hours before had been spent in intense preparation. The leaders of the two waves, Lieutenant Commanders K. W. Williamson and J. W. "Ginger" Hale, reviewed the latest Maryland photos, taken that morning and flown over from Malta in a Swordfish. Just at dusk, a Sunderland flying boat overflew Taranto and radioed that not only was the Italian fleet still in port, but a sixth battleship had just anchored.[3]

The Taranto harbor has two main areas: the Mar Grande, a circular basin three miles wide and about forty-five feet deep, separated from the sea by breakwaters and San Pietro Island; and an inner harbor, the landlocked Mar Piccolo. The two are joined by a canal. The battleships and large cruisers were moored in the former; the inner harbor held smaller cruisers, destroyers, and many other lesser craft and was surrounded by seaplane hangars, storage sheds, and fuel tanks. Williamson, commanding the first wave, decided that part of his group would approach the harbor from the west at 9,000 feet, drop to sea level, crossing the Diga di Tarantola, and launch their torpedoes at the *Cavour,* while the other half of his flight would come in from the northwest, giving the antiaircraft defenses two things to think about at once.

Hale, leader of the second wave, chose to take his entire flight in from the northwest, then turn south, to increase the chances of hitting a battleship as the targets overlapped each other at this angle. The drawbacks of Hale's approach were the concentration of antiaircraft guns at the nearby canal and the row of almost invisible barrage balloons. The chances were against hitting a balloon cable, however, as the cables were 900 feet apart and the plane wingspans were 48 feet.

The torpedoes were equipped with duplex pistols, or detonators, which would ignite either on contact or on passing under a steel hull, set off by the magnetic field generated by the ship. These new detonators tended to explode prematurely in a rough sea, however, and needed to run at least 900 feet before the safety latch was deactivated. They also needed to be dropped level, at slow speed, from an altitude of 150 feet or less. No fancy evasive maneuvers, not too close, not too far—the plane had to fly straight and level, a perfect target for an antiaircraft gunner.

Each aircraft carrying bombs was armed with six 250-pound bombs, and the planes scheduled to drop illuminating flares each carried four bombs and sixteen flares. The planes from the *Illustrious* bore the letter L, while those from the *Eagle* were marked with an E.[4]

In the hour before takeoff, as the Ionian Sea darkened, the observers were up in the Air Intelligence Office getting a last briefing and studying the most recent photographs. It was their job to navigate across the Gulf of Taranto to their target, and then return, tired and perhaps wounded, and locate their ship.

The term *observer* is a bland one that fails to convey the necessary level of skill or the position of trust occupied. In 1940, if the observer was the senior officer, he, and not the pilot, commanded the flight. Consider his duties and the picture becomes clearer.

In 1940, navigation was still mostly a manual skill. The *Illustrious* had a radio homing beacon and both surface and air radar, all quite new, but navigating the skies in 1940 was only a little different from navigation in Columbus's day. The observer read a compass, consulted his watch, and noted the air speed. He noted the outside air temperature, the altitude, and the barometric pressure, all of which could affect the performance of the instruments. A drift meter gave the speed and direction of crosswinds. He calculated wind triangles to determine the true course and speed. He observed the sun or, at night, the stars to calculate position. He had to use paper and pencil and a flight calculator with a 100-knot wind screaming through his workplace and a flame roaring from the the exhaust pipe a few feet from his ears.

Navigating in such a manner, the Fleet Air Arm observer had to find a tiny steel rectangle, often obscured by mist and clouds, in a great ocean, as the fuel ran low. But navigation was not his only duty. He was also trained in reconnaissance. He had to memorize the appearance of hundreds of ships. In a brief opening through the clouds, he might have only a moment to identify the nationality of a ship or a fleet (and in the excitement and confusion of war, it is easy to mistake friend for foe), to count the number and type of each vessel, and to estimate their speed and direction. In addition, the observer needed to know how to operate the radio (if no radioman was aboard), fire the tail gun, and identify enemy airplanes. Certainly pilot and observer needed each other on this and every flight.

In the hours before takeoff on that evening of November 11, down below on the hangar deck, the Swordfish were crowded together, their wings folded like immense resting dragonflies. The fitters checked everything within reach and then moved the still-folded planes, one at a time, onto the narrow elevator and up onto the deck, where the wings were swung forward and locked into place. By now the stars were out, intermittently obscured by high, scudding clouds.

At 8:00 P.M., the final plane of the first wave was on deck. The commander (flying) looked down on the dim scene below him, where the pilots and observers in their bulky suits and flotation vests, assisted by the deck crew, were climbing into their cockpits and firing up the engines. The exhaust manifolds glowed red as the motors warmed, and tongues of blue and orange flame flicked at the tips of the exhaust stacks.

The roar of the motors rose above the hiss of the bow wave and the whine of the wind through the ship's rigging. Far below, the boiler room artificers opened additional burners; more steam raced into the turbines, and the great hull cut through the night-shrouded water at more than thirty knots.

The pilots scanned their dials, and the observers clipped their navigation boards into place and settled their earphones over their heads. Then the sudden glow of a green flashlight from the flight deck officer signaled that all was ready. The commander (flying) gave assent in a controlled voice, the green light on the flying bridge glowed, the deck crews pulled back the chocks, and one at a time the first wave roared down the deck and into the star-filled sky.

Far ahead of them, Taranto was experiencing its first disturbance of the night. A diaphone had heard a distant plane. The alarm was sounded, the civilians ran to air-raid shelters, and the antiaircraft batteries fired a few shots at random. Ten minutes later, the commotion died away. An hour later, the alarms rang again. This time, it was the patrolling Sunderland flying boat that passed high overhead—unmolested, as the Italians had no night fighter planes—and flew away to the south. Peace descended once again.[5]

The Swordfish pilots were fairly comfortable, droning along at 4,000 feet, headed northwest, but each observer shared his cockpit with a huge auxiliary gasoline tank that displaced him to the seat usually reserved for the gunner. Twenty minutes into the flight, clouds obscured the sky, the moon dimmed, and all was dark. The leaders were flying blind on instruments, with up and down, left and right only an abstraction on the dials. Twenty minutes later, at 7,000 feet, they broke into the clear. Below was a white ocean of mist, above were the stars. Williamson saw seven other planes, but four were somewhere else in the vast sky. Nothing could be done. There were no plane-to-plane radios, and he could only hope that the missing Swordfish were still headed for Taranto.

Over their left shoulders shone a quarter moon, not bright enough to clearly show the Italian ships, but enough to suffuse a pale glow into the carpet of clouds below.

At 10:50 P.M., the air-raid alarm at Taranto sounded a third time. The tired civilians trooped into basements once again, as the gun crews scanned the sky once more. Now many planes could be heard, somewhere off toward the south. Even before their targets were identified, the gun crews began to fire into the sky wildly, apparently at the noise made by one of the missing torpedo craft, L4M, piloted by Lt. H. A. I. Swayne, with Sublieutenant A. J. Buscall as observer. They had arrived thirty minutes ahead of their comrades and had amused themselves by flying in circles while awaiting the other Swordfish.

The approaching planes saw a great array of colored lights over Taranto, rising 10,000 feet high—splashes of blue, red, green, and orange, with brief winks of silver—ten cubic miles of flying bullets, flaming tracer shells, and hot, jagged steel fragments.

And that was exactly where they were headed.[6]

# Chapter Ten

➤

# Volleyed and Thundered

As the rest of the first wave caught up with Lieutenant Swayne, it was clear that any element of surprise was long gone. Certainly, every citizen of Taranto was wide awake.

Thus far, only the land-based batteries were firing. Hundreds more guns waited, silent, aboard the battleships, cruisers, and destroyers in the dark harbor; over half of the guns had yet to fire a single shot. Yet on the Swordfish flew, into the heart of this inferno.

The habits of practice and the discipline of long training guided each pilot as he went to his allotted place. The two flare-dropping planes flew off at 7,000 feet along the northeast shore of the Mar Grande and deposited a line of parachute flares, one every half mile, their brilliant blue-white light outlining the great ships at anchor, as the other planes swarmed out to the west and began their long, diving torpedo runs.

All the torpedo planes were carrying Mark XII torpedoes, eighteen inches in diameter, set to run at a speed of twenty-seven knots at a depth of thirty-three feet. Each torpedo had a tiny propeller on the nose, which had to turn a certain number of revolutions in order to arm the detonator. All the torpedoes the night of November 11 were set to run 300 yards before they would explode on contact. This meant that if the torpedoes were launched closer than 300 yards, if they struck their target, they might make a dent but would not explode.

The first plane in was that flown by Lieutenant Commander Williamson. He passed over San Pietro Island at 4,000 feet, flew southeast parallel to the outer breakwater, and then dived low over the Diga di Tarantola, barely missing a balloon cable, skimmed past two destroyers that fired at him from almost point-blank range, and released his torpedo at the *Cavour* from a height of about 30 feet. As he banked sharply to starboard, a burst of machine gun bullets tore his plane, and it plunged

73

into the water near the floating dock. Amazingly, he and his observer, Lt. N. J. Scarlett, survived the crash and, after being punched about by the dock workers who fished them out of the harbor, were taken as prisoners of war. (To their surprise, however, the Italian military people treated them almost as heroes, plied them with cigarettes, and two nights later, during an RAF bombing raid, entertained them in the bomb shelter with a rendition of "Tipperary.") Williamson's torpedo narrowly missed the destroyer *Fulmine* and struck the *Cavour* between the bridge and B turret; 24,000 tons of battleship began to settle onto the muddy floor of the harbor.[1]

The next two planes, piloted by Sublieutenants P. D. J. Sparke and A. S. D. Macaulay, followed a parallel course, a few hundred feet to the north. They passed untouched through the same hailstorm of bullets and sent both their torpedoes toward the *Cavour,* but missed. Both torpedoes ran on half a mile farther and exploded near the *Doria,* causing no damage. Sparke and Macaulay banked sharply to port, circled back over the outer harbor, and in three minutes were in the comparative safety of the gulf sky, heading home.

Next in was Lt. N. M. Kemp, who crossed the submerged breakwater north of San Pietro Island at 4,000 feet, under fire by gunners on the island, on the antiaircraft barges near the breakwater, and on nearby Point Rondinella. As he neared the city of Taranto, he banked sharply to starboard and dived between Taranto and the row of anchored cruisers, which opened an intense barrage as he leveled out just above the waves. He observed that some of the heavy shells fired by the Italian cruisers struck merchant ships anchored nearby in the harbor. Ahead of him, outlined against the silver light of the flares, was the vast bulk of the *Littorio.* Kemp held his course steady until the distance had narrowed to 1,000 yards, dropped his torpedo, pulled into a steep climb, and after three minutes of wild evasive action was also droning south in the quiet night sky. Kemp's torpedo ran true and opened a hole forty-nine feet long and thirty-two feet wide on the starboard bow of the *Littorio.*

Lt. H. A. I. Swayne, who had arrived early over Taranto and witnessed the onset of the wild fireworks display that still filled the sky, followed in after Kemp, but at 1,000 feet and to the south of the cruiser anchorage, making a steep left turn through gusts of tracer fire, he flew in over the northern tip of the Diga di Tarantola and came at the *Littorio* from the opposite side. Swayne dropped his torpedo only 400 yards from the target, pulled up enough to clear the masts of the battleship, and got away over San Pietro Island under heavy fire from the cruisers and shore batteries.

Soon he was following Kemp to the empty skies over the open sea. His torpedo struck the *Littorio* on the port quarter, folding back the steel plating in a gap twenty-three by five feet, just a few seconds after the first torpedo had struck home. The *Littorio* began to settle nose first into the mud.

The final torpedo-armed Swordfish of the first wave, flown by Lt. M. R. Maund, had experienced a difficult time during the trip to Taranto. Like the others, the cold night air whistling through the open cockpit had chilled the pilot and his observer, Sublieutenant W. A. Bull, to the bone. Climbing steeply into the clouds in an attempt to find the others, Maund barely missed another Swordfish, but he regained his position with the flight. When the reassembled flight had left the clouds behind and were out in the clear night air, they could see the gray coast to starboard, dim in the moonlight. No sooner had they settled back on their course than they noticed the fiery display ahead of them, and they were soon in it themselves. Maund came in from the northwest, over the land of Point Rondinella, and made his run through renewed bursts of tracer. He could look down into the back gardens of houses below, illuminated by the moon and the dazzling row of flares two miles ahead.

Now he turned south toward the battleship area, dipping and weaving as wildly as could be done with almost a ton of torpedo slung between the wheels, desperate to throw off the hailstorm of flak, the tracers of every color, coming from every direction. Suddenly a battleship, probably the *Veneto,* loomed ahead at a distance of 1,300 yards, filling his torpedo sights. The plane rose as the torpedo plunged into the water, and Maund made his dash past the bridges and funnels of a fleet of merchant ships, using them as a shield against the ever more frantic fountains of tracer. One moment they were only fifty yards from the pom-pom guns of a destroyer. The gun crew was so startled that they did not fire until he was off again, dipping and wheeling just off the water. He flew, throttle full open, past the black bulk of San Pietro Island, which erupted in fire from every point. Then, suddenly, over the deep waters, he was safe. The torpedo, oblivious to the effort invested in its delivery, missed the *Veneto* and exploded harmlessly off the starboard quarter of the *Littorio.*[2]

There were four other planes in this first wave, two with bombs and flares and two with bombs only. Capt. O. Patch (Royal Marines) had as his target the cluster of destroyers in the Mar Piccolo. He dived from 8,000 feet through a torrent of fireballs to about 200 feet, released his six bombs, and pulled out, heading for the unlit countryside to the east. Antiaircraft fire from yet another position caused Patch to dive behind a range of hills, navigating just above the trees by the light of the moon. All six of his bombs either missed the target or did not explode.

Sublieutenant W. C. Sarra dove from 8,000 feet to 1,500 feet but had difficulty identifying his target on the Mar Piccolo. As he passed over the dockyard, he saw the hangars of the seaplane base (where Admiral Lyster had been stationed twenty years before) and released his bombs. There was a large explosion at the aviation facility, and as Sarra flew out over the dark land eastward, the burning hangars lit the horizon.

Sublieutenant A. J. Forde, who had become separated from the flight on the way to Taranto, arrived just as the flares were illuminating the harbor. Turning northeast over Cape San Vito, he headed for the dockyards, turned to port, and attacked, flying toward the southwest, dropping his bombs from 1,500 feet, but scored no hits. His first bomb fell in the water, just short of a heavy cruiser. All the way down, he had been under intense antiaircraft fire, but after his first run, he could not be sure that all of his bombs had released, so he turned around over the western part of the Mar Piccolo and repeated the attack, still under heavy fire. He headed away toward the north, crossed the coast about five miles west of the harbor, and started home.

The final plane of the first wave, piloted by Lt. J. B. Murray, arrived just to the east of Cape San Vito while flares were being dropped, and flew north to the extreme eastern end of the inner harbor. Murray dropped his bombs from 3,000 feet and landed one on the destroyer *Libeccio,* but the bomb failed to explode and produced only a ragged hole. He made a steep turn to port, flew away into the eastern sky, and then made his course toward the *Illustrious.*[3]

Long after 11:30 P.M., when the last plane of the first wave had departed, the defenders continued to fill the sky with flak bursts and streams of colored tracer.

Far south of Taranto, the *Illustrious* had been launching the nine planes of the second wave, led by Lt. Comdr. J. W. "Ginger" Hale. This time, things did not go smoothly. As the final two planes proceeded to the center line of the deck, they locked wings. The pilots stopped their engines and the fitters pried the wings apart. One plane was apparently undamaged, but L5F had torn fabric and two broken ribs in one wing. After brief consultation, L5Q, thought to be whole, took off and joined the circling flight, which had been puzzling over the tardy pilots. The bridge flashed a Morse signal, "Carry on," and the eight planes flew north while L5F was lowered to the hangar deck with her crew pleading for a rapid repair.[4]

There must have been undetected damage to L5Q, because thirty miles from the carrier, its auxiliary gas tank fell off, and the loose fittings began banging against the fuselage. (L5Q was carrying bombs, not a torpedo, and hence was equipped with an external long-range tank.) The engine stopped briefly, and the pilot, Lt. W. D. Morford, dived to keep his speed up, switched to an internal tank, and restarted his motor.

On his return to the *Illustrious,* he and his observer, Sublieutenant R. A. Green, were greeted by antiaircraft fire. Approaching the carrier, they had displayed a red flare, but as they were not expected, both the *Illustrious* and the cruiser *Berwick* opened fire. Morford flew out of range and fired a two-star identification light, was recognized as a friend, and landed safely.

Meanwhile, Hale and his remaining seven planes were headed north at 8,000 feet. A little after 11:00 P.M., they spotted the vast pyramid of light over the harbor, the sum of innumerable shells and bullets, visible far at sea. The Italian listening devices soon detected the incoming second wave, and the batteries redoubled their frenzy of firing long before the planes came within range. Close to midnight, just south of the Mar Grande, Hale detached his two flare-dropping planes, flown by Lieutenants R. W. V. Hamilton and R. G. Skelton, and sent them along the eastern shore of the harbor; their observers dropped twenty-four flares, and a brilliant magnesium glare again lit up the whole harbor. Then Hamilton and Skelton made a run over the oil storage depots, where their bombs started a fire. As they departed the area, the antiaircraft batteries gave them a tremendous send-off but made no hole in either plane.

The other five aircraft, each carrying a torpedo, crossed to the north shore, then turned southeast toward battleship row. Hale led off, diving from 5,000 feet, jinking from side to side to confuse the Italian gunners, all of whom were firing so continuously that their gun barrels glowed red. As he passed over the merchant ship anchor area, the air above the harbor reeked of acrid smoke. Hale leveled off at thirty feet above the water, selected the *Littorio,* and dropped his torpedo at a range of 700 yards. Evading the hundreds of guns firing at him by a wild climbing turn to starboard, he skimmed past a balloon cable, avoided the fire of several more batteries, and joined the others heading south toward Cephalonia's waiting waters. His torpedo tore a third hole in the *Littorio,* thirty feet wide and forty feet long, at the very bottom of the hull.

Next in was Lt. G. W. Bayley and his observer, Lt H. J. Slaughter. They headed over the cruiser area and were not seen again that night. The Italian records state that a plane crashed near the cruiser *Gorizia.* Bayley's body was found the next day; Slaughter was never found.

Lt. C. S. C. Lea came in after Hale, but not liking the flak concentration, made a 360-degree turn to lose altitude and came in under the area of the heaviest tracer activity. As he skimmed over the water, the *Duilio* loomed ahead in his torpedo sight. The torpedo ran true and hit the *Duilio* on the starboard side thirty feet below the waterline, blowing a hole thirty-six feet long and twenty-four feet high. As the water poured in, the crew ran her up on the beach to prevent her sinking. Lea made his escape at water level, barely missing a fishing boat, skimming between the cruisers *Zara* and *Fiume,* who fired on each other as he passed through the space between them. Soon he too was away to safety.

The Swordfish flown by Lt. F. M. A. Torrens-Spence also began its run in from high above Point Rondinella, diving toward a point just south of the inter-harbor canal. Torrens-Spence was the last person to see Bayley and Slaughter, as their planes nearly collided in the fiery confusion. Soon Torrens-Spence was skimming the waves in the midst of many huge ships, all of which were firing at him. He pointed his Swordfish at a very large ship, probably the *Veneto,* launched his torpedo, then began wild evasive maneuvers, swooping and turning, at one point even dipping a wheel into the water of the harbor. Flying at an altitude of three feet, he suddenly saw a steel barge anchored in front of him, covered with antiaircraft guns. They fired at him just as he pulled up, close enough to feel the heat of the muzzle blasts, but by astonishing good fortune, he escaped into the night with a single, harmless bullet hole in the fuselage. His torpedo either missed or was defective, as it had no known effect.

E5H, piloted by Lt. J. W. G. Wellham, staggered off the deck loaded (like the other planes) with a maximum weight, including the torpedoes and the long-range tank, found his leader, and took up formation. They set course flying for Taranto at about 7,000 feet. The flight was uneventful, but even thirty miles away from Taranto, Wellham could see the vast display of tracer fire. As he arrived over the harbor, it became apparent that with the intensity of the flak and general confusion below, there was very little chance of a coordinated attack. His group split up, and Wellham aimed for an area where there appeared to be relatively less antiaircraft fire, over the west side of the harbor. He began his dive and met a barrage balloon at the height of 4,000 feet (no tethered balloon could have been at this altitude; its cable must have been shot away). To avoid a collision, he made a violent maneuver, almost standing the aircraft on its nose, which much alarmed his observer.

As he recovered from this sudden maneuver, he felt a powerful blow on the control stick and found that he could not lift the port wing. At the moment, it was impossible to tell what had gone wrong, other than that they had been hit and something was jammed. In a twin-engine plane, it might have been possible to adjust the throttles to give more power to one side, but this was not possible for the pilot with only one engine. Wellham's only alternative was to try to free the jam by slamming the stick hard in each direction, pulling it back and forth, while opening and closing the throttle, hoping that these unusual stresses would free the aileron. This worked to some extent, and he regained partial control of the airplane.

The aircraft had been losing altitude all the while, and he suddenly realized that he was diving straight into the city of Taranto. He pulled the plane into a right turn and flew over the north side of the harbor. His aircraft would fly straight only with one wing slightly down and skidding. As he leveled out at 100 feet above the sea, the horizon behind him to his right appeared completely blocked by an enormous battleship, later identified as the *Vittorio Veneto.* He swung the tail of the plane back and forth to reduce speed and leveled the plane to regain the correct attitude for torpedo dropping. The air was full of tracers, and it seemed that every antiaircraft gun in Taranto was being fired at him. Most of the shells were passing above him. When he dropped his torpedo, the Swordfish, suddenly released from a ton of burden, immediately rose, putting him right up into the flak. His plane was hit a second time but continued to fly. Zigzagging wildly between ships to spoil the gunners' aim, he was soon outside the breakwater and began to climb into the now bulletfree night sky.[5]

His observer, Lt. Pat Humphries, ever a help in crucial moments, said calmly and quietly over the intercom, "That was a bit exciting while it lasted. I think that you have bent the airplane somewhat. Do you think she will get us home?" Wellham replied with a tentative affirmative, and Humphries gave him a course to steer. After what seemed a long time, Wellham inquired about their progress, and Humphries replied that they were thirty miles from the *Illustrious,* as he had just picked up the homing beam. They did not need to alter course, and they found the carrier without difficulty. Wellham switched on his lights and commenced the landing approach, at which point troubles started again.

As soon as he throttled back to the correct speed for deck landing, the aircraft became uncontrollable. The deck landing control officer was very experienced and realized that there must be some reason why Wellham was approaching so fast, so he gave him a very early signal to cut the engine. E5H landed with a thump and picked up an arrestor wire. The flight deck crew quickly led the plane forward onto the aircraft elevator and folded the wings. As they descended into the brilliantly lit hangar, Wellham could see why his Stringbag had not been flying very well. The port aileron rod was in two jagged pieces, useless for moving that control surface, and in the port lower mainplane there was a hole about a yard long and half a yard wide. Inside the hole could be seen the remains of several shattered wing ribs. The sturdy Swordfish had flown more than 100 miles with damage that would have brought down a lesser craft. As for Wellham's torpedo, it had had no effect; with the damaged controls inducing a wing-down, skidding flight, he had probably dropped his torpedo badly.

Meanwhile, back on the *Illustrious,* L5F has been lowered ignominiously into the hangar with two broken wing ribs and torn wing fabric. Her pilot, Lt. E. W. Clifford, and observer, Lt. G. R. M. Going, pleaded with the fitters and riggers to do the impossible: fix the plane in time to join the others at Taranto. It was 9:50 P.M. By 10:10 P.M., the skillful repair crews had replaced the broken ribs, cut out the ripped fabric, and doped new fabric into place, and the plane was ready to fly. The commander (flying), with some considerable doubts, gave his permission, and off Clifford and Going went into the night.

When they arrived at Taranto, flying at 8,000 feet, only twenty-four minutes behind their companions, they had a splendid view of the maelstrom of fire and color that filled the harbor that evening, the event still known in Italian history books as *La Notte di Taranto*—Taranto Night.

Far below, the last of the Swordfish were flying away from the harbor. The dying flares and the orange glare from the burning hangars illuminated great slicks of leaking oil spreading over the harbor. Clifford descended to 2,500 feet and flew in circles, looking for a proper target. Docked in the inner harbor was the high-speed cruiser *Trento.* Clifford did a wingover, dropped 2,000 feet straight down amid a furious flurry of pom-pom tracer shells, and released his six bombs.

As he pulled out and flew north across the Mar Piccolo to the sheltering dark of the countryside, his observer saw no explosions, and they felt that their attack had been a failure. In fact, the bombs were defective (not unusual in that era), and although one had punched a large round hole in the deck of the *Trento,* it had not exploded.

With Clifford's departure, the skies over Taranto were empty, with only a few flashes where batteries were still firing at wisps of smoke and imagined engine noises.

In the two hours of Taranto Night, the Italian shore batteries had fired 1,430 125-millimeter rounds, 313 107-millimeter rounds, 6,854 88-millimeter rounds, 931 40-millimeter rounds, 2,635 20-millimeter rounds, and 638 8-millimeter rounds—a total of 12,800 projectiles. There are no figures on the number of rounds fired by the gun crews aboard the ships, but 15,000 is not unreasonable. For every hit, the defenders fired an estimated 8,000 rounds.

Back at the *Illustrious,* the hours crept by. The reconnaissance photos had shown clearly the numerous guns, the new balloons, and the three torpedo nets. What could twenty planes do against such a vast fleet in such a well-protected harbor? Perhaps it had been a mistake. Perhaps none of the planes would return and those young faces would never again be seen by their comrades, by their families. There was nothing to do but wait.

The pilots, for their part, high up in the dark night sky, had a few worries as well. Those who had escaped being hit by antiaircraft fire had the usual work of navigating through a trackless sky, using their primitive instruments, and of setting a plane down on a carrier deck at night when fatigued. But there was an even more ominous possibility: Suppose the carrier and her escorts had been attacked by Italian surface forces, cruisers, destroyers, or torpedo boats that had been missed by navy intelligence or patrols.

If so attacked, the order given to the *Illustrious* and her escort force was, "If enemy surface forces are encountered during the night, *Illustrious* is to withdraw, remainder are to engage under C.S. 3. Two destroyers are to be detailed to withdraw with *Illustrious.*" In such event, the pilots might return to the rendezvous spot and find no aircraft carrier.

The rendezvous time was 1:00 A.M. At the agreed position, the *Illustrious* came up into the wind and put on steam for twenty-one knots. And waited. But the sky was empty, the radar screen blank. The minutes went by. Men looked at their watches. Then at 1:12, a blip appeared on the radar screen, then another, then many.

The fire and crash teams swarmed up onto the deck, followed by the riggers and fitters. The surgeons switched on the lights in their surgery room, ready for the first casualty. At 1:20, L4C touched down, followed by all the other members of the first strike except Williamson and Scarlett, who by this time, unknown to their comrades, were in dry clothes on the Italian destroyer *Fulmine,* chatting with their none too happy hosts.

Only one aircraft lost out of twelve; that was surprisingly good news. There was no need to wait for the second wave, as "Ginger" Hale in L5A was already circling to land, followed shortly by six more planes of the second wave. Almost an hour later, Clifford and Going, whose damaged plane had been the last to depart, switched on their lights, circled the carrier, and came to rest. Bayley and Slaughter were missing and by now would have run out of fuel if they were still flying. Each wave had lost one plane, but it was not clear how much had been accomplished.

As in all warfare, there had been death. The British had lost two men, and the Italians had lost twenty-three aboard the *Littorio,* sixteen on the *Conte di Cavour,* and one on the *Duilio.*

With the noise and darkness and confusion, and from the modest reports of the pilots, it was difficult to determine overall success. But the Marylands from Malta and their photographs would tell the story.

Lt. J. W. G. Wellham, Royal Navy, before receiving the Distinguished
Service Cross, aboard HMS *Eagle,* Alexandria, Egypt, in 1940. After a role
in the movie "Find, Fix, and Strike," he decided that aviation, not the
cinema, would remain his metier. *John W. G. Wellham and Fleet Air Arm
Museum negative #PERS/30.*

Lieutenant Campbell "batting on" a Fairey Swordfish aboard HMS *Biter* in August 1944. Note arresting hook forward of the tail wheel. *John W. G. Wellham and Fleet Air Arm Museum negative #SWFH/291.*

HMS *Eagle* photographed over the tail of a Swordfish of 824 Squadron in the Eastern Mediterranean in 1940. Aircraft of 813 and 824 Squadron are on the deck. The *Eagle* was laid down to be a Chilean battleship in 1913 then bought by the Admiralty and completed as an aircraft carrier. She was Commander Wellham's home for several years. *John W. G. Wellham and Fleet Air Arm Museum negative #CARS E/15.*

Swordfish E5H practicing torpedo dropping. The "tin fish" weighs 1,600 pounds. *John W. G. Wellham and Fleet Air Arm Museum negative #SWFH/588.*

Commander Wellham's Swordfish in the Western Desert of Egypt being repaired after Italian bullets put holes in the engine cowling and the main spar, nicking Wellham's ankle. The damage occured August 22, 1940, during the raid on Bomba, Libya, when three Swordfish sank four Italian warships. *John W. G. Wellham and Fleet Air Arm Museum negative #SWFH/528.*

The high-speed Martin Maryland bombers flying out of Malta kept close watch on the fleet at Taranto. This one is being serviced in the Western Desert. *Smithsonian Institution negative #13919 A.C.*

Italian bomber Savoia-Marchetti SM-79 was nicknamed "The Hunchback" because of the cupola behind the pilot. This one carries a torpedo destined for the British fleet. *Bundesarchiv, Koblenz negative #415 1624 4A.*

HMS *Illustrious* in June 1940. When *Eagle* was forced to withdraw after bomb damage, Swordfish launched from *Illustrious* carried the entire burden of the Taranto attack. Six months after this photo, German planes put 7,000 pounds of bombs through her flight deck. *John W. G. Wellham and Fleet Air Arm Museum negative #CARS I/171.*

The Mar Piccolo (inner harbor) twenty-four hours after the attack. The cruisers *Trieste, Bolzano,* and *Trento* are leaking fuel oil, shown by swirls of discoloration in the water. *Fleet Air Arm Museum negative #TARANTO/3.*

The channels between the Mar Piccolo (above) and the Mar Grande (below), three days after the attack. A small vessel still leaks oil (upper right), and a battleship (lower center) is attended by repair craft. The photo aircraft was at 16,000 feet. *John W. G. Wellham and Fleet Air Arm Museum.*

An Italian battleship, her bow underwater and her keel in the mud, is attended by eleven rescue vessels, including a submarine, which provides electric power. Oil still discolors the harbor. *Fleet Air Arm Museum.*

| | DATE | Type | No. | 1ST PILOT | OR PASSENGER | (INCLUDING RESULTS AND REMARKS) | DUAL (1) | PILOT (2) | DUAL (3) | PILOT (4) |
|---|------|------|-----|-----------|--------------|----------------------------------|----------|-----------|----------|-----------|
| | – | – | – | · | – | — TOTALS BROUGHT FORWARD | 67.20 | 657.05 | 1.40 | 22.3 |
| | 2. | SWORDFISH | K8419 | SELF. | LT. HUMPHREYS, L/A. WILLS. | A/S PATROL. | | 2.25 | | |
| | | "EAGLE SQUADRON", H.M.S. ILLUSTRIOUS. | | | | | | | | |
| | 7 | SWORDFISH | P4070 | SELF. | LT. HUMPHREYS L/A. FERRIGAH. | A/S PATROL. 1st LANDING WITH BARRIER: 16 KNTS. OVER DECK: DAMAGED TAILWHEEL. | | 2.35 | | |
| | 9 | SWORDFISH | P4070 | SELF. | LT. HUMPHREYS. L/A. FERRIGAN. | SEARCH: FOUND ATAK: GAVE POS. OF FLEET: FOUND CANT. 2501 IN SEA: (SHOT DOWN BY FULMARS EARLIER), 2 MEN ALIVE: PROC. WITH SEARCH. FAILED TO FIND FLEET. SQUARE SEARCH: N.B.S: O/E. RET. SAFELY. LANDED IN PARK | | 4.65 | | |
| | 10 | SWORDFISH | P4206 | SELF. | LT. HUMPHREYS. N/A. BALDWIN. | A/S. PATROL: N/A. | | 2.40 | | |
| | 11/12 | SWORDFISH. | P4949 | SELF. | LT. HUMPHREYS. | ATTACK ON ITALIAN BATTLE FLEET IN TARANTO HARBOUR: ARRIVED TARGET MIDNIGHT. FLEW OVER TOWN AND BASE. H.A. POOR, MET BARRAGE BALLOON AT 7000' (PROB. ADRIFT.): DIVED THRU INTENSE L.A. BARRAGE. HIT BY M.G. BULLETS. PENNT. PLNR. STRUT SMASHED. FORM. LT. BLOWN OFF. INT-MIL.ROD. DAMAGED. OUT OF CONTROL FOR 500': DROPPED FISH ON PT. QUTR. OF "LITTORIO" PROD.HIT. TURNED TO STBD. HIT BY EXPL. BREDA BULLETS IN PT. MN.-PLN. SPAR SMASHED GOT AWAY SAFELY. RET. TO "ILLUST." LANDED. O.K. RESULTS OF RAID:- 3 BATTLE-SHIPS OUT OF ACTION. 2 CRUISERS & 2 FLEET AUXLRS. SINKING. SEAPLANE HANGAR AND DOCKS DAMAGED.— NOT BAD! | | .55 | | 4.0 |
| | | Awarded Mention in Despatches (3rd). | | | | | | | | |
| | | FLT. 824 (E.) SQUDN. DISEMBARKED H.M.S. NILE II. DEKHEILA. | | | | | | | | |
| | 20 | SWORDFISH | P4206 | SELF. | LT. HUMPHREYS. | BEACON TEST. ABSOLUTELY NO. RESULTS. | | .10 | | |
| | 28 | SWORDFISH | K8419 | SELF. | S/LT.(A) WOOLLEY. L/A. WILLS. | TO EAGLE. OUTER. A/S. NO HAPPENING. | | 3.20 | | |

German bombs explode on and around HMS *Illustrious* in Grand Harbor, Valletta, Malta. The already-damaged carrier survived the further assault, escaped to Suez at night, and was rebuilt in the United States. *Fleet Air Arm Museum negative #CAMP/415.*

| | DAY | | | NIGHT | | ENGER | | |
|---|---|---|---|---|---|---|---|---|
| | 1ST<br>PILOT | 2ND<br>PILOT | | | | | DUAL | PILOT |
| AL | (6) | (7) | (8) | (9) | (10) | (11) | (12) | (13) |
| | | | | DAY. | NIGHT | | | 16·10 |
| | 35·20 | | | 171 | 3 | 30·25 | 10·00 | |
| | | | | 1 | | | | |
| | | | | 1 | | | | |
| | | | | | 1 | | | 1·30 |
| | | | | 1 | | | | |
| | | | | | 1 | | | |
| | | | | | | | | |
| | | | | | | | | |
| | | | | 1 | | | | |

A page from Commander Wellham's flying log noting the attack on Taranto, the damage to his plane, and the presence of his observer, Lieutenant Humphreys. The previous entry notes the rescue of two Italian aviators. *Commander Wellham's collection.*

Enormous seas and freezing gales batter HMS *Searcher* as she guards a convoy en route to north Russia. Two Grumman Martlets are on the flight deck, with Swordfish in the hangar below. *Fleet Air Arm Museum negative #CARS S/31.*

A Japanese admiral and other senior officers visited Taranto in May 1941, six months before Pearl Harbor. Here they discuss the British raid with senior Italian naval officers, on the deck of the battleship *Littorio*. *Italian Navy Historical Office.*

A Japanese "Kate" torpedo bomber (Nakajima B5N). Kates sank many British and American warships. A high-level armor-piercing bomb from a Kate destroyed the USS *Arizona* at Pearl Harbor. Kates tended to burst into flame when hit and were obsolete by 1943. *Smithsonian Institution negative A48649.*

This dramatic photo of Battleship Row was taken from a Japanese plane after the torpedo attack but before the dive-bombers struck. The oil slicks, reminiscent of Taranto, are already spreading from shattered fuel tanks. *U.S. Naval Historical Center negative #NH 50472.*

"Val" (Aichi D3A) dive-bombers en route to attack Pearl Harbor. Vals were as agile as most fighter planes in 1940 and sank more ships than any other dive-bomber in World War II. *National Archives negative #80-G-167384.*

December 7, 1941. American failure to anticipate the Japanese attack was dramatically underscored by the explosion of the forward magazine of the USS *Shaw*. The forward turrets of *Nevada* are silhouetted against the sheet of flame. *U.S. Naval Historical Center negative #NH 86118.*

## Chapter Eleven

> ➤

# The Morning After

By 3:00 A.M., AFTER THE LAST SWORDFISH HAD RETURNED, THE *ILLUSTRIOUS* was steaming south to avoid shore-based bombers and four hours later joined Cunningham's main force. Cunningham's flagship flew signal pennants that meant, "*Illustrious,* maneuver well executed." The other flag halyard bore pennants meaning, "All ships—repeat signal Admiral is now flying." This is the greatest honor any ship can receive in the British Navy. Three Cant Z.-501 seaplanes approached the fleet that morning, but all were shot down by radar-vectored Fulmars.

Lyster, upon reviewing the pilots' preliminary reports, decided that the attack should be repeated the coming night, before the Italians had time to improve their defenses. Cunningham had some doubts about the soundness of sending the handful of exhausted pilots back into the inferno of Taranto. (One pilot, when queried, said, "After all, they only asked the Light Brigade to do it once.") But he deferred the decision to Lyster. The matter was settled, however, as a storm blew in and foul weather, headwinds, and poor visibility put an end to any thoughts of a second raid.[1]

Meanwhile, on the Italian side, the Operations Room of the Supermarina in Rome had been calling for details all night, but Admiral Riccardi and his men were too busy rescuing damaged ships and putting out fires to file lengthy reports. Salvage tugs and repair parties scurried about doing their best to put things right.

The sun rose on a scene of confusion and destruction. The *Littorio's* bows were underwater as a result of the three huge holes in her hull, and divers found an unexploded torpedo just under her. Herculean efforts by the Italian shipyard workers were to restore the *Littorio* to service in five months. The *Duilio's* number one and two magazines were completely flooded, and she had to be beached to avoid total loss. She would be repaired and returned to service in six months.

Salvage crews tried to tow the *Cavour* to shore to beach her, but the pumps could not stay ahead of the water pouring in from damaged bulkheads, and at 5:45 A.M. she was abandoned; by daybreak, she had settled quietly to the bottom with the whole of her decks underwater. She was not refloated until July 1941 and was still under repair at Trieste when the war ended. The inner harbor was awash with oil from the fuel tanks of the *Trento,* which had been cracked by the unexploded bomb, and many bulkheads and ventilation ducts were ruptured. Months were required to remedy the damage.[2] Near misses had fractured the bow of the destroyer *Libeccio* and the hull of the destroyer *Pessagno.* The remains of the seaplane base were still burning at noon. Several hangars were only twisted skeletons of blackened steel. Broken seaplanes littered the taxi apron and the ramp into the harbor.

Small craft crossing the Mar Grande that morning found the body of Lieutenant Bayley; he was buried by the Italians with full military honors in the cemetery at Taranto. His observer, Lieutenant Slaughter, was never found.

Count Galeazzo Ciano, Italy's minister for foreign affairs and son-in-law of Mussolini, noted in his diary on November 12: "A black day. The British, without warning, have attacked the Italian Fleet at Taranto and have sunk the dreadnought *Cavour* and seriously damaged the battleships *Littorio* and *Duilio.* . . . I thought I would find the Duce downhearted. Instead, he took the blow quite well and does not, at the moment, seem to have realized its gravity."[3]

The professional men of the Italian command had no difficulty in seeing the implications of *La Notte di Taranto:* It meant that their naval aerial reconnaissance was poorly managed by the Regia Aeronautica; that their reconnaissance planes lacked sufficient speed, altitude, and armament to survive a trip over the British fleet; that their antiaircraft fire was woefully inaccurate (true for most countries in 1940); and worst of all, that their best harbor, their harbor closest to the sea lanes of the Mediterranean, was not secure. The day following the raid, the two undamaged battleships, *Vittorio Veneto* and *Giulio Cesare,* moved north to Naples, which rendered them safer but of little use militarily.

And certainly Taranto demonstrated that the battleship had become obsolete. Churchill was slow to grasp that, and the United States chose to keep battleships in active service until 1992. The American choice, while strongly endorsed by the U.S. Navy, was criticized by some commentators as a political move more than a military one.

On November 13, 1940, the *New York Times* noted an Italian Navy communiqué of the previous day that announced that one Italian warship had been damaged in an air raid on Taranto harbor and that the Italians had shot down six British aircraft and seriously damaged three others. Whether this assessment was an intentional lie or simply reflected the confusion of the night is unclear, but what the Marylands of Malta photographed at Taranto could not be disputed.

On the morning of November 12, Flight Lieutenant Whitely and his Maryland crew departed from Malta, flew over Corfu near the Greek coast, and then headed west, a direction from which the Italians at Taranto were not expecting him. He had been unaware of the previous night's raid and was startled to see one battleship partly submerged and another beached, and the harbor dense with oil and debris. While his observer was taking photos, his radio operator sent a message in code summarizing their observations, but Whitely felt that no coded communiqué could give sufficient scope to the drama of the scene below, so he sent a second, uncoded message describing in dramatic terms the smoke, confusion, and damage that filled the Taranto basin.[4]

Taranto affected the hearts and minds of those involved. Italian morale, often precarious, sank low, and the hard-pressed British felt a new confidence in their ability to survive and prevail.

The same day as the Taranto raid, the Italian Air Force struck across the English Channel in a raid on the Medway. A force of twelve Fiat BR-20 bombers and forty Fiat CR-42 fighters were met by thirty Hawker Hurricanes. The Italian losses were heavy; British losses were nil. Churchill remarked that the Regia Aeronautica might better have stayed home, defending Taranto.

Several days after the Taranto raid, almost unnoticed in the confusion and destruction, a slight figure in an unfamiliar uniform studied Taranto harbor intently, inquiring about depths and distances, making careful notes. This was Lt. Takeshi Naito, assistant air attaché at the Japanese embassy in Berlin. The implications of those sunken battleships were not lost to him.[5]

# Chapter Twelve

>

# ABC Equals Z

THE LESSONS OF TARANTO, TAUGHT BY ABC CUNNINGHAM AND HIS men, were not equally well understood. Some politicians and military men instantly grasped the implications, while others could not comprehend that a new age was upon them. And some saw a clear link between Taranto and Pearl Harbor, even though twelve thousand miles separated the two harbors.

In 1940, Adm. Joseph O. Richardson, commander of the American Pacific Fleet, objected to his being based at Pearl Harbor, which he saw as very vulnerable to an attack by Japanese carrier-based aircraft. When he raised questions about siting the main fleet at Oahu, Adm. Harold R. Stark, chief of naval operations, told Richardson that the purpose of having the fleet in Hawaiian waters was to deter Japanese aggression. This did not a seem good enough explanation, and Richardson carried his objections to President Roosevelt at a White House luncheon on October 8, 1940. Next month, almost exactly on Taranto Night, Richardson was fired for going out of channels and was replaced at Pearl Harbor by Adm. Husband E. Kimmel.[1]

News of Taranto, carried by every newspaper in the world, made a deep impression on Secretary Knox of the U.S. Navy. The defense of Pearl Harbor was the responsibility of the U.S. Army, and Knox wrote to Secretary Stimson in the War Department (the cabinet post that controlled the U.S. Army in 1940). Knox stated clearly that Taranto was a warning of what could happen if Japan should launch a surprise attack upon Pearl Harbor and urged that antitorpedo defenses be rushed into place and that more radar and interceptor planes be provided. The army replied that it was fully aware of its responsibilities and that the harbor defenses were already better than adequate.[2]

What seems even more astonishing is a letter of February 15, 1941, sent by Admiral Stark to Admiral Kimmel, commander in chief of the

U.S. Pacific Fleet. In this communication, Stark asserted that torpedo nets were unnecessary at Pearl Harbor because "A minimum depth of seventy-five feet may be assumed necessary to successfully drop torpedoes from planes." It would seem that Admiral Stark was unaware of the attack on Taranto, three months earlier.[3]

In January 1941, Ambassador Joseph Grew, American representative in Japan, sent a secret cable to the State Department warning that Tokyo was awash with rumors of an impending surprise attack on Pearl Harbor, using all Japanese resources. The State Department routed the cable to the Office of Naval Intelligence, where it was reviewed by Comdr. Arthur H. McCollum, chief of the Far Eastern Section, who rather curtly informed the State Department that these rumors were totally unfounded and that no attack on Pearl Harbor seemed planned or likely.[4]

The man who seems to have learned the most from Taranto was Isoroku Yamamoto; for him, it was decisive proof that his concepts were sound. Another event, which occurred halfway around the world, in the Indian Ocean, and took place on the same day as the Taranto raid, cast a whole new light on future Japanese plans.

The German raider *Atlantis,* commanded by Capt. Bernard Rogge and disguised as a Dutch freighter, captured the British freighter *Automedon.* Aboard the British vessel was Capt. M. F. L. Evans, a special Admiralty courier bound for Singapore. He carried a valuable sealed pouch destined for commander in chief, Far East; in it was the chiefs of staff decision that Singapore could not be defended, would receive no fleet increase, and must be written off. The *Atlantis's* sudden attack knocked Captain Evans unconscious, and all of his documents were quickly read by Lt. Ulrich Mohr. Rogge steamed at top speed for Japan. On December 5, 1940, the documents were at the German embassy in Tokyo; within seven days, all the relevant officers in Berlin and Tokyo had translations.[5]

Now Yamamoto knew for certain at least two things: a fleet in a shallow harbor could be sunk by carrier attack, and he could ignore the British fleet at Singapore. This, combined with the December 15, 1940, survey of the Taranto harbor wreckage, done by two German officers, Baron von Gronau and Col. John Jebsen and fowarded to Tokyo, set his mind at ease about both the feasibility and the safety of an attack on Pearl Harbor. He could throw the major portion of his carrier forces east against Hawaii without worrying about major British reinforcements coming from India or the Mediterranean. Yamamoto now turned his full attention to Operation Z.

Until now, the planning for an attack on Pearl Harbor had rested mostly in Yamamoto's mind and included three seemingly fantastic assumptions: that the American fleet would cooperate by lying peacefully in harbor at the time of attack; that six huge Japanese aircraft carriers, refueling at sea from tankers and accompanied by a fleet of battleships, cruisers, and destroyers, could cross the Pacific Ocean and come within 200 miles of Honolulu totally undetected; and that an attack involving 6 aircraft carriers and 350 warplanes could be coordinated without breaking radio silence.

These were serious considerations, and in early February 1941, Yamamoto sought the opinions of his colleagues. In a letter to Rear Adm. Takajiro Onishi, chief of staff of the Eleventh Air Fleet, Yamamoto enclosed his plan of attack and asked for review and comment. Onishi, in turn, requested the opinion of Minoru Genda, a young, brilliant pilot recently promoted to commander. After the war, he became head of the Air Force in Japan's American-approved "Self-Defense Force". Genda had already proved himself as a student of attacks on anchored fleets: He had been assistant air attaché in London at the time of the Taranto raid and had prepared a report sent to Japanese naval intelligence describing the British raid.

Genda locked himself in his room on the carrier *Kaga* and studied the plan for ten days. He examined every assumption, recalculated all the data, considered every contingency, reviewed the one relevant historical precedent, Taranto, and rendered his opinion: It would be difficult, but the plan stood a reasonable chance of success.

Within a month, the Combined Fleet staff and several sections of the Naval General Staff were at work, planning the thousands of details. Many experienced pilots were called back from the war in China and set to practicing dive-bombing and low-level torpedo attacks. Genda himself was named chief of staff of Operation Z, to organize the tactical implementation of the master plan.

The Japanese consulate in Honolulu, where a very competent spy masqueraded as an obscure clerk, was asked to obtain photos of the plan of anchorage of the navy ships in Pearl Harbor. No hidden cameras were needed; the agent went to a souvenir shop and bought a number of postcards showing aerial views of Pearl Harbor, with ships in place, and sent them to Tokyo via the diplomatic pouch. Copies of these postcards were in the cockpit of each attack plane on December 7, 1941.

This spy, Takeo Yoshikawa, age 29, was a graduate of the Japanese naval academy at Eta Jima. Retired early because of stomach trouble, he was recalled to duty in 1937 and given four years of intensive English lessons. On March 27, 1941, the *Nitta Maru* docked at Honolulu and Yoshikawa came ashore. For the next eight months, he seemed more a tourist than a consular clerk. He favored a teahouse on Alewa Heights, which overlooks Pearl Harbor. The owner kept a telescope on the balcony for the convenience of customers. In May, Yoshikawa took a glass-bottom boat ride across Kaneohe Bay and confirmed that it was too shallow for a fleet anchorage. That same month, he traveled to Maui and confirmed that the fleet no longer used the Lahaina anchorage. The airport at Honolulu offered tourist flights over Oahu; in September, he took a geisha friend on a scenic flight that covered every part of Pearl Harbor. Yoshikawa's two most useful discoveries were that the fleet was in port every Sunday and that departing air patrols never seemed to go north.

On November 15, 1941, American intelligence picked up a coded radio message for Yoshikawa. When it was decoded on December 3, the text included the words "relations most critical . . . harbor report twice a week . . . extra care to maintain secrecy."

The Japanese Navy, of course, relied on far more than tourist postcards and flights with geishas. Under the direction of Kanji Ogawa, chief of Section 5 of the Third Bureau (Intelligence) of the Naval General Staff, a vast and splendidly organized file had been created with details of fleet equipment, personnel, schedules, and habits. As an example, in early December 1940, the U.S. Navy decided that the traditional anchorage off Lahaina on the island of Maui was unsatisfactory, and the fleet began to move to Honolulu. This information was received in Tokyo, evaluated, and forwarded to the fleet by Ogawa well before the end of December.

After clarifying the details of the Pearl Harbor anchorages, the next issue was determining when the American fleet would be in harbor. Yamamoto's long experience with American bureaucracy, the reports coming in from Honolulu, the status of the U.S. fleet as "training" not "wartime," and, perhaps, the well-known tropical languor induced by the gentle climate of Hawaii all suggested that the U.S. Navy would not deviate from its habitual pattern of "fleet in port Saturday morning and shore leave on Saturday night." This would mean, of course, that Sunday morning would find the crews sleeping or hung over.

Then there was the necessity of crossing 4,000 miles of ocean without being noticed. All commercial ships use certain well-known paths, usually a great circle course, to minimize the consumption of fuel. Yamamoto planned to steam well north of the customary shipping lanes, refuel at sea (still a very new skill), and then head south, crossing a spot 500 miles from Honolulu at sunset. A full night of high-speed steaming would put him 200 miles from Pearl Harbor at sunrise, at a spot rarely visited by American patrol planes.

A report sent to Washington, D.C., in August 1941, prepared by Rear Adm. Patrick Bellinger and Maj. Gen. Frederick Martin (responsible for Hawaiian air defense), predicted that Japan would attack Pearl Harbor before a declaration of war, using planes and submarines, and that the aircraft carriers would cross the North Pacific in the "empty" areas away from shipping lanes. The same week, the chief of naval operations in Washington predicted that Japan would attack on a Saturday or a Sunday.[6] Astonishingly, no effective use was made of these reports.

Yamamoto considered several factors in the British raids and compared them with his own situation. When the Swordfish planes had arrived at Taranto, the war was already well under way, the harbor was on full alert, the ships were prepared to make steam, and the antiaircraft guns were not only ready but firing. By contrast, the Japanese would be attacking a nation at peace, with few defenses manned. (And in fact, because of bureaucratic concerns for inventory control and possible sabotage, many of the American ammunition lockers at Pearl Harbor were padlocked, and when the Japanese planes appeared, the personnel with the keys were unavailable.)

Next was the matter of torpedoes. The British standard-issue torpedo, the Mark XII, was eighteen inches in diameter, ran fairly slowly, and needed to be launched in a smooth sea at ninety knots, from 150 feet or less above the water. Even when launched properly, many failed to function. At Taranto, for example, of eleven launched, only five torpedoes hit and detonated. At Pearl Harbor, it is unclear what percentage of the torpedoes ran true, but certainly enough to blast holes in most of the American capital ships. (Although the Japanese had oxygen-powered torpedoes, they seem to have used air-powered ones at Pearl Harbor, since aerial photos show long trails of bubbles marking the torpedoes' wakes.)

In the year before Pearl Harbor, the Japanese had puzzled mightily over how to launch torpedoes in shallow water. (They do not seem to have been aware of the British wire cable technique.) Launched conventionally, torpedoes may sink as deep as 200 feet before assuming their preset running depth. Pearl Harbor has an average depth of 40 feet. A torpedo stuck in the mud is of little use. Genda and Mitsuo Fuchida set their pilots the difficult task of launching torpedoes from a height of 40 feet at 150 knots. This low and slow technique reduced sink depth somewhat but was a hazard to the pilots. During September 1941, the torpedo technicians at Yokosuka, experimenting with wooden fins attached to the torpedoes, succeeded in launching torpedoes in 36 feet of water, shallow enough for Pearl Harbor.[7]

A new frustration arose. The planned attack date was nine weeks away, but only 30 of the new torpedoes were available, not enough for practice. The final 150 would not be ready until November 30, when the fleet would be headed across the North Pacific. Desperate efforts were made to speed production. When the Japanese fleet sailed for the rendezvous at Hitokappu Bay, many torpedoes were still unfinished. The *Kaga* stayed behind, loaded the unfinished weapons and their technicians, and steamed north as scores of men labored below decks, completing their task. The completed torpedoes were distributed to the fleet hours before sailing time. History tells us that enough were available on December 7, 1941, and that they ran very well indeed in shallow water.

Fuchida, in a television interview in *The World At War,* stated, "The most difficult problem was launching torpedoes in shallow water. The British Navy attacked the Italian fleet at Taranto, and I owe very much for this lesson in shallow-water launching."

The link between Fuchida and Taranto is more direct than might seem likely at first glance. In October 1941, Takeshi Naito, now a lieutenant commander, still had vivid memories of his flight from Berlin to Taranto and his inspection of the harbor eleven months earlier. After his Taranto trip, Naito had discussed his findings with Minoru Genda, who was then in London.[8]

Naito and Fuchida were old friends and had been classmates at Naval Staff College and at Kasumigaura Air Station. On the afternoon of October 23, 1941, Naito and another Japanese officer, who had just returned from Germany in August, gave a lecture to Yamamoto's staff. Present was Mitsuo Fuchida, who was slated to lead the aerial attack on Pearl Harbor. After the briefing, Naito stayed overnight at the Kagoshima naval facility. The next day, Fuchida spent many hours interrogating his friend about Taranto. Naito was not within the closed circle privy to the plan regarding Pearl Harbor; if he sensed the reason behind Fuchida's interest, he never betrayed it.[9]

An even more powerful indication of Japan's interest in Taranto was the visit of a large, high-level delegation to Italy from May 18 through June 8, 1941, just six months before Pearl Harbor. The dignitaries included Rear Adm. Koki Abe. Vice Adm. Giuseppe Fioravanzo, later director of the Italian Navy's Office of History, was appointed as host for the visiting Japanese delegation. Fioravanzo recalled that they arrived with an enormous list of detailed questions: "The Japanese showed great interest in the aerial torpedo attack against the ships anchored at Taranto the night of November 12, 1940." The many photographs from Fioravanzo's collection show Japanese and Italian officers of high rank saluting, posing for group portraits, and chatting seriously, all on the decks of ships in Taranto harbor. (Adm. Renato Sicurezza, current chief of history for the Italian Navy, writes that from the navy's records, they are not currently able to name the persons in the photos.)[10]

Certainly some U.S. Navy men were thinking along the same lines as the Japanese regarding shallow-water torpedo attacks. On June 13, 1941, Rear Adm. Royal Ingersoll sent a memo to all naval district commanders in which he called attention to British and American successes in shallow-water torpedo dropping. He noted that in the past, seventy-five feet had been considered the minimum depth for torpedo work, and suggested that now "no minimum depth of water in which naval vessels may be anchored can arbitrarily be assumed as providing safety. . . ." Ingersoll concluded by citing Taranto.[11]

The Japanese further compared their task with the British raid on the Italian fleet. For the attack on Taranto, ABC Cunningham had had only one aircraft carrier, the *Illustrious.* Yamamoto would have six carriers: the *Akagi, Kaga, Soryu, Shokaku, Zuikaku,* and *Ryujo.* The *Illustrious* had been able to successfully launch 21 planes toward Taranto; the six Japanese carriers would hold 350 planes.

To assault Taranto, the British had had the Swordfish, a plane with many virtues but already of another era—a remarkably effective antique but an antique all the same. Yamamoto's plan included the use of three different airplanes. In the first wave would be dive-bombing specialists, flying the Aichi D3A1 (American code name Val), an all-metal monoplane with dive brakes and fixed wheels. The Vals would be followed by Kates, carrying torpedoes. The Kate (Nakajima B5N2) was a very effective, well-designed torpedo bomber with hydraulically operated retracting landing gear (many planes in 1940 had gear that the pilot had to crank into place manually). Finally, air cover would be provided by the Mitsubishi A6M, soon to be universally known as the Zero. American intelligence experts were to be unpleasantly surprised by the quality and performance of the Val, the Kate, and the Zero.[12]

By June, Yamamoto and his staff felt that their chances of success were even greater than that of the Swordfish pilots at Taranto. Compared with the British efforts, the Japanese had better planes, better torpedoes, seventeen times as many planes, and the enormous advantage of attacking a nation not only at peace but apparently half asleep.

Further, Commander Genda had solved the problem of coordinating an attack without breaking radio silence; in fact, he learned it from watching a newsreel film of American carrier maneuvers. Unlike the Japanese practice of dispersal, where 100 miles separated carriers, the American ships stayed within sight of each other and communicated by signal lamps. Within a week, fresh Japanese maneuvers showed this to be practical. It seemed that every obstacle to Japanese success had been overcome.

Still, the Imperial Naval General Staff did not agree with Yamamoto; they thought the operation was far too risky. But on July 25, 1941, the American president, in an attempt to restrict the Japanese conquest of China and Southeast Asia, expanded the American trade embargo to include oil. On July 26, the British also stopped oil sales to Japan, and Holland followed suit the next day. Japan, almost devoid of native petroleum, considered the alternatives and decided in early September to invade the oil-rich Dutch East Indies. Everything else followed from this decision: If there were to be petroleum-powered vehicles, they would need tires, which would call for rubber. British Malaya produced rubber. As the Philippines lay between Japan and Malaya, an attack on the Philippines would be necessary, but this would bring the United States into the war. Japan knew that its only possible hope of defeating the United States lay in eliminating the American Pacific Fleet during the first hour of the conflict.[13]

At 7:00 A.M. on December 7, 1941, Commander Fuchida, leading a wave of forty-nine Kates carrying armor-piercing bombs, picked up a commercial radio weather report of clear skies over Pearl Harbor. He readjusted his course, using the Honolulu radio station as a homing beacon. Forty minutes later, he was over Pearl Harbor. He observed the quiet harbor, the empty roads, the blue sky without a single opposing plane. He counted the battleships.

Then he slid back his transparent cockpit canopy and unholstered his flare gun. The pilots had been briefed on the flare signals: One flare meant that the attackers had achieved surprise and that the torpedo planes would go in first; two flares meant that there was opposition and that the dive-bombers and fighters would lead the way.

Fuchida fired a single flare. There was no opposition, no American P-40s diving out of the sun, no ugly bursts of flak reaching up for the Japanese bombers. Pearl Harbor, in that final, fleeting moment, was still asleep.

## Chapter Thirteen

➤

# Applying the Hard Lessons

ALL OVER THE WORLD, A WHOLE GENERATION OF SENIOR NAVAL
commanders, steeped in a long tradition of battleships, gunnery, and armor
plate, was learning to use the new dreadnought of a dawning age: the
aircraft carrier. Flexibility, mobility, swiftness, boldness, and surprise
were the issues now, rather than just slugging it out with broadsides.

After Commander Fuchida fired his flare, the world changed, and
America was dragged center stage out of its isolationism. Fuchida's flare was
the signal for 181 Japanese aircraft—fighters, dive-bombers, and torpedo
planes—to begin their attack. Between 8:00 and 8:30 the morning of
December 7, 1941, they torpedoed American ships and bombed and
strafed military facilities all over Oahu. At 9:00, a second wave of 170
more Japanese planes appeared over Pearl Harbor. By the time the last
plane flew north to rejoin the Japanese fleet, Pearl Harbor and a dozen
other nearby facilities were in flames. Six battleships were sunk; two
battleships, three cruisers, and three destroyers were badly damaged; and
128 American planes were damaged and 180 were totally destroyed; and
3,600 American men were killed or wounded. At Kaneohe Naval Air
Station and Ewa Marine Air Station, not a single plane remained usable,
and except for the carriers that were at sea, the U.S. Pacific Fleet was
no longer operational.

The evening of December 7, 1941, as Adm. Chuichi Nagumo's
strike force turned for Japan, he radioed Yamamoto of the great victory.
But for Yamamoto, elation was tempered by the knowledge that not
one American carrier had been scratched, and they, not the battleships,
had been the real targets sought at Pearl Harbor.

Taranto and Pearl Harbor had both been milestones, hard lessons in
the classroom of war, but five months after Pearl Harbor came the action
that shaped naval affairs for the next generation, changed the course of

the war even further, and showed how swiftly the tide of war could now turn: the Battle of Midway.

As Japanese victories in Malaya, Singapore, Guam, the Philippines, and the Dutch East Indies stunned the world, Yamamoto, back home, continued to press for action to the north against the American carriers. His concerns evoked little support until April 18, 1942, when sixteen twin-engine B-25 bombers, launched from the *Hornet,* attacked Tokyo. Little real damage was done, but the emperor had been threatened, and there was no longer any opposition to Yamamoto's plan for destroying the American carrier fleet at Midway.

While the Imperial Japanese Navy prepared for this vast operation, the first carrier-versus-carrier battle in history was fought May 7, 1942, in the Coral Sea. The opposing surface ships never saw each other. On the Japanese side, the *Shoho,* a small carrier, was sunk; the *Shokaku* went home for repairs; and the *Zuikaku* lost so many planes that she had to withdraw until new aircrews became available. The United States lost the *Lexington,* and the *Yorktown* limped away, burning and badly damaged. (The Japanese believed that the *Yorktown* had been sunk.)[1]

### FORCES AVAILABLE MAY 6, 1942, FOR THE BATTLE OF MIDWAY

|  | Japan | United States |
|---|---|---|
| Battleships | 11 | 0 |
| Carriers | 8 | 3 |
| Cruisers | 22 | 8 |
| Destroyers | 65 | 15 |
| Submarines | 21 | 19 |

The table above indicates the sea power that Yamamoto could muster for the Midway operation. He planned an invasion of Midway, which was to draw the American carriers out where they could be destroyed. In this plan, he divided his forces into five groups: an advance force of sixteen submarines, deployed between Honolulu and Midway, to report the arrival of the U.S. carriers; a northern force, with two light carriers, which would lure part of the American fleet away through an attack on Alaska; a force of four large aircraft carriers, which would bomb Midway's defenses on June 4, 1942; an invasion force of troop transports, battleships, and other large warships, which would occupy Midway the day after the air attack; and the main body, centering around Yamamoto's flagship, the superbattleship *Yamato,* and ten other battleships, which would wait east of Midway until the Americans entered the trap and then crush them.

It was a splendid plan as long as the Americans cooperated. But they did not.

Adm. Chester Nimitz and his crews had more than courage and determination—they had a brilliant team of code breakers, who decoded large portions of the Japanese radio traffic.

By early May 1942, radio intercepts showed that a massive Japanese effort was under way, but the target was identified only by its code name, AF. Comdr. Joseph J. Rochefort had an idea, and on May 10 he arranged for Midway to send a radio message that there was a fresh water shortage. Two days later, a Japanese signal mentioned that "AF was short of fresh water." Now Nimitz knew the place, and other signals had given the approximate time—three weeks. But to meet this onslaught, Nimitz had no battleships (most were still in the mud at Pearl Harbor) and no carriers. The *Lexington* was sunk, the *Saratoga* was at San Diego training new crews, the *Enterprise* and *Hornet* were in the South Pacific, and the *Yorktown,* full of bomb holes, was headed for Honolulu.

The *Enterprise* and *Hornet* were ordered north at top speed. The *Yorktown* limped into Pearl Harbor on May 27. Surveyors said it would take three weeks to fix her. Nimitz gave them three days, but a force of 1,400 skilled workers, welding and fabricating around the clock, did the job in two and a half.

Nimitz sidestepped two of the five Japanese battle groups: He ignored the attack on Alaska, and moved his carriers north before the Japanese submarine cordon was in place. Then he put every available bomber, fighter, and antiaircraft gun onto the island of Midway. The runway at this desolate atoll was spotted with an assortment of B-17s, B-26s, Catalinas, Avengers, Wildcats, Dauntlesses, Vindicators, and Buffaloes.

At 9 A.M. on June 3, a flying boat out of Midway spotted the Japanese transport fleet and its escort. Nine B-17s attacked the convoy that afternoon. This was their first combat; they dropped thirty-six bombs and missed with every one. That night, four Catalina flying boats made a low-level torpedo attack, which damaged an oiling vessel.

The following day, between 5:00 in the morning and 5:00 in the evening, American naval aviators changed the course of history. The advantage ebbed and flowed from minute to minute. The complexity of events and the mounting danger seized both sides and held them in a grip that even fifty years later is difficult to describe.[2]

At 4:30 A.M., the four Japanese carriers launched the first strike: thirty-six Kates from both the *Hiryu* and *Soryu* and thirty-six Vals from both the *Akagi* and *Kaga*. All were armed with bombs. As they flew east toward Midway, the remaining Kates were armed with torpedoes and sat on the flight decks, ready to attack the American carriers when they were located. Some Zeroes went with the outgoing bombers, and others circled over the carriers for defense. At about 5:40 A.M., a Catalina reported both the approaching bombers and the Japanese carriers.

An American interceptor group of obsolete Wildcats and antique Buffaloes met the attack, but they were nearly all destroyed by the superior Zeroes. At 6:31 A.M., 108 Japanese planes began to bomb and strafe Midway. Although damage was heavy, the principal targets—American bombers—were absent; alerted by radar, they had flown east out of danger. At 7:00 the Japanese attack leader radioed that a second strike was needed.

Here was Nagumo's first dilemma. Two of his four carriers had their decks covered with torpedo-loaded Kates. If he found the U.S. fleet in the next few minutes, he could launch his fully ready Kates. If he was to attack Midway instead, he must unload the torpedoes and replace them with bombs. At 7:10, an American torpedo attack by six Avengers and four B-26s made up his mind. Although the Americans were shot down and scored no hits, one falling B-26 passed a few feet overhead, terrifying those on Nagumo's bridge. Nagumo ordered the Kates taken below and switched from torpedoes to bombs. As this process was well under way, a Japanese search plane reported seeing the American fleet. Nagumo reversed his orders: Take the bombs off and put the torpedoes back. The sweating hangar crews worked furiously, but there are limits to what men can do.

At 7:30, two American carriers were launching planes toward Nagumo, as American bombers from Midway were beginning another attack. Between 7:55 and 8:20, forty-two American planes from Midway approached the Japanese carriers; nearly every plane was shot down, and not one scored a hit. The Japanese were feeling increasingly confident.

At 8:20, as the last American plane was plunging into the sea, Nagumo learned that American carriers were nearby. At the same moment, the first wave of Kates, Vals, and Zeroes returning from Midway began to arrive, their gas tanks almost empty. They had to be landed. The overhead cover of Zeroes was also low on fuel, and the combat-ready Kates were armed at this point with a mix of bombs and torpedoes.

If Nagumo launched now, his available bombers would have no

fighter escort and would lack the torpedoes needed for an effective attack on the American carriers. If he did not launch, he must put his armed planes down below again and quickly land the almost fuelless first wave.

He made his decision: Delay the attack until 10:30, stow all the armed Kates, land the first wave, refuel and rearm all his planes, and launch an all-out, coordinated effort when he was completely ready. At 9:20, this activity was in full swing, when the first carrier-based American torpedo planes arrived. Enough Zeroes remained on patrol to massacre the U.S. Navy planes. In the next sixty minutes, three whole squadrons of American fliers were shot down, and still not one Japanese carrier had been hit.

Nagumo felt a renewed surge of confidence. The sea was littered with American wreckage. His full attack force was almost ready to launch, and his fleet was intact. His intelligence reports told him that the Americans had only two carriers, and he had seen with his own eyes that most of the carrier-based American planes were gone. It was 10:22 A.M.

But this was the high-water mark for the Japanese Navy. In the furious defense against the low-level torpedo attacks, the Japanese lookouts (they had no radar) had failed to notice some specks high in the sky. These specks grew rapidly, as two full squadrons of Dauntless dive-bombers dropped vertically upon Nagumo's ships.

The first bomb that hit the *Akagi* set off an inferno of burning gasoline and exploding torpedoes. The rudder jammed full over, and electrical power failed. It was finished. At the same moment, four bombs hit the *Kaga*. The first flash of flame killed everyone on the bridge. Though it took the *Kaga* nine hours to sink, she was no longer a fighting ship. The *Soryu* was hit at 10:25 and burst into flames. When the fire reached the torpedo storage room, an enormous explosion rocked the ship.

In one hour, the Americans had lost most of their planes and the Japanese had lost three of their four carriers.[3]

But the *Hiryu* remained untouched. At 10:58, she launched every available plane at the Americans. An hour later, her Vals put three bombs into the *Yorktown,* blowing a hole in the deck, setting a huge fire, and stopping the engines. At 1:30 P.M., a second wave from *Hiryu,* mostly planes from the three burning carriers, which had found a new home on the *Hiryu,* put two torpedoes into the *Yorktown,* and at 3 P.M. the *Yorktown* was abandoned.

At 2:30, an American scout plane had located the Hiryu. At 5 P.M., dive-bombers from the *Hornet* and *Enterprise* arrived. The *Hiryu* burned for fifteen hours before finally sinking. It was over. The Japanese main force, with its eleven battleships, had not fired a shot. Yamamoto, with every carrier gone, turned home.

The disaster was concealed from the Japanese public for years. The families of the wounded were not allowed to visit; the surviving carrier men were kept isolated. But to the admirals on both sides, it was no secret that aircraft carriers, not battleships, would rule the seas.[4]

Taranto had shown that battleships could be sunk in heavily defended shallow harbors, even by a handful of attackers. Pearl Harbor, building on the lessons of Taranto, had demonstrated that the same could be done even more thoroughly by a larger attacking force, striking a less-defended harbor. Midway was a deep-water demonstration that huge ships, and the fleet that depended on them, could be destroyed by aerial attack, with the added advantage that the stricken ships sank too deeply to ever be salvaged. Battleships, those great fire-breathing dragons, had passed into history.

## Chapter Fourteen

➤

# The Summing Up

ANY COMPARISON OF TARANTO AND PEARL HARBOR MUST INCLUDE THE specifics of both the antiaircraft defenses and the machines used to make the attack.

At Taranto, the shore-based antiaircraft guns included 21 batteries of 102-millimeter guns, 84 heavy machine guns, and 104 light machine guns. All were put on full alert at nightfall. As for ship-based antiaircraft guns, the battleship *Littorio* had her 12 88-millimeter guns and 40 .50-caliber machine guns. In the harbor, in addition to the *Littorio,* there were five other battleships, nine cruisers, twenty-eight destroyers, sixteen submarines, and five motor torpedo boats, all with modern antiaircraft guns in numbers proportional to the size of the vessel. Standard orders, as issued by the base commander, called for all shipboard antiaircraft guns to be fully manned at nightfall and kept on full alert. The Italian antiaircraft guns, manned and ready to fire that night, numbered close to 1,000. After the actual attack, all the British pilots agreed that the air was filled with tracer bullets and exploding ack-ack.[1]

At Pearl Harbor, the first line of defense should have been radar, which had been fully operational in Great Britain before the end of 1939, linked to a series of fighter control centers, and crucial in the Battle of Britain. Although American scientists had full knowledge of radar technology and had provided four radar units for Hawaii, because of interdepartment rivalries and inertia in the army bureacracy Hawaii's radar went unused.

Once the Japanese passed the radar net, they had to face the guns of Pearl Harbor. But none of the shipboard guns had been manned at 7:00 that Sunday morning, no crews were on alert, and much of the ammunition was locked up for inventory control. This sorry state of preparedness reflected the division of responsibility in American defense: The army was responsible for defending the navy's harbor. And in accordance with the orders of Lt. Gen. Walter C. Short, most of the ammunition for the shore-based army antiaircraft guns was locked in Aliamanu Crater Depot, several miles from Pearl Harbor. (Short was afraid that the Japanese-American citizens of Honolulu would seize the ammunition.) The army's fixed antiaircraft batteries had been issued a very limited supply, which was kept in boxes somewhat nearer the guns, but the mobile antiaircraft guns, in general, had no ammunition.

Col. William J. Flood commanded Wheeler Field, where fifty P-40s, the army's best fighter planes, stood ready to defend Hawaii. Colonel Flood had arranged the construction of more than 100 dirt revetments, with walls ten feet high, dispersed around the periphery of the field to protect his precious fighters. General Short's orders, however, were to line up the planes, wingtip to wingtip, just in front of the hangars, in order to more easily guard them from saboteurs. For the same reason, the ammunition was removed from the planes each evening and stored elsewhere. When Lt. Tomatsu Ema flew over Wheeler Field, he saw no antiaircraft fire at all and later remarked, "It was more like a practice run than actual combat."[2]

The shipboard navy gun crews, most awakened from sleep or hangover, rushed to their stations and tried to rescue an already desperate situation. The antiaircraft guns mounted on the ships in Pearl Harbor, as of 7:00 A.M. on December 7, 1941, numbered as follows: 276 five-inch guns, 4 four-inch guns, 51 three-inch guns, 56 1.1-inch guns, 8 six-pounders, 6 three-pounders, 2 one-pounders, 20 twenty-millimeter guns, 12 forty-millimeter guns, and 112 machine guns.[3]

The confusion, surprise, and damage of the first moments of the attack greatly reduced the number that actually did fire. Many of the guns, especially the three-inch ones, were obsolete, and most had their ammunition in locked storage.

The army-manned shore-based antiaircraft guns were close to non-existent. Wheeler Field, crucial to the defense of Hawaii, had no antiaircraft guns other than a few machine guns, and these were unmanned at the time of the attack, with the ammunition locked up and no earthworks to protect the crews if they had been present.[4]

The antiaircraft success stories at Pearl Harbor were those of brave and desperate men, not those of an organized, professional military defense. The 55th Coast Artillery set up machine guns in a tennis court and began to fire. Two marines at Ewa shot down a Japanese plane using the tail gun of a dive-bomber that was parked by the airstrip. An army man with a hand-held Browning automatic rifle shot down a low-flying plane, but even in the second wave of the attack, when all American forces were mobilized, no more than eight of the planes shot down could be attributed to antiaircraft fire, and the larger number was the result of the few American fighter planes that struggled into the air that morning to do battle with the attackers. In fact, the American antiaircraft gunners shot down almost as many American planes as they did Japanese ones.

There are many stories of prompt and effective response by American enlisted men and junior officers. The crew of the *Pennsylvania* opened fire by 8:05, even though the ship was in dry dock. The *Tangier* shot down three Japanese airplanes. The *Grebe* had her two three-inch guns dismantled for overhaul, and the crew fired rifles and pistols, downing one Japanese bomber. The gunboat *Sacramento* had her guns manned by 8:00 A.M. and hit two planes.[5]

At Taranto, the shore-based defenders had fired 12,800 rounds at the British planes, while the ships' crews fired thousands more. The number of rounds fired by the American defenders at Pearl Harbor will never be known, however, because of the complete confusion that morning and the destruction of records in the fires and explosions.[6]

And what about the attacking craft in those two raids? The table on the next page compares the Fairey Swordfish, used for both dive-bombing and torpedo work, with the Val and the Kate. The Val was a specialized dive-bomber, whereas the Kate was designed for both torpedo dropping and horizontal high-level bombing but not dive-bombing. (The table clearly indicates that the two Japanese planes were faster, longer-ranged, and capable of reaching higher altitudes than the Swordfish. From anecdotal evidence, the Swordfish seems to have better survived damage.)

From the professional pilot's point of view, each plane had its own personality. The Swordfish was almost as maneuverable as a fighter plane, very light on the controls, hard to stall or spin, and very stable in a dive.[7] And there were other advantages to the relative slowness of the Swordfish besides easy landing. In combat, enemy gunners tended to aim too far in advance, assuming that the Swordfish was moving faster than it was.

The Kate seemed to be free of faults, being stable on takeoff and landing and easy to recover from stalls and spins; however, it lacked self-sealing gas tanks, burned easily when hit, and was too slow for combat by 1943. Kates sank the *Lexington, Hornet,* and *Yorktown,* as well as many of the battleships at Pearl Harbor.[8]

The Val, based on German designs, sank more ships than any other dive-bomber in World War II. Although twice as fast as the Swordfish, it could carry only half the weight of bombs. In level flight, it was pleasant to fly. During a dive, the dive brakes were very effective in speed control, but a steep dive produced violent juddering and vibration. In a very steep dive, or in any rapid maneuver, such as a steep turn, both hands were required to move the control stick, unlike the Swordfish, which responded easily and smoothly.[9]

| | Fairey TSR Swordfish | Aichi D3A Val | Nakajima B5N2 Kate |
|---|---|---|---|
| **Type** | **Dive–Bomber Torpedo Bomber** | **Dive–Bomber** | **Torpedo Bomber Horizontal Bomber** |
| *Top Speed level flight m.p.h.* | 154 | 240 | 216 |
| *Bomb load pounds* | 1,500 | 880 | 1,600 |
| *Ceiling in feet* | 11,000 | 30,000 | 24,000 |
| *Torpedo load pounds* | 1,600 | N/A | 1,700 |
| *Number built* | 2,391 | 1,495 | 1,149 |
| *Still flying 1994* | 2 | 0 | 0 |
| *Maximum range (nm)* | 600 | 800 | 1,900 |

*Published figures vary. Range varies with speed and use of auxiliary tanks. Speed varies wih load carried.*

At Taranto, the British sent in 21 planes and 2 were shot down, a 10 percent loss rate. At Pearl Harbor, the Japanese sent in 350 planes and lost 29, a loss rate of 8 percent.

At Taranto, the British sank three battleships, damaged a cruiser and three destroyers, and destroyed the seaplane base. At Pearl Harbor, the Japanese sank or severely damaged eight battleships, three cruisers, three destroyers, and four smaller auxiliary craft. At the U.S. Navy seaplane base at Kaneohe, all of the thirty-six Catalina patrol planes were destroyed except for three that were out on patrol, and the hangars were burned. At Hickam Field, Wheeler Field, Bellows Field, Haleiwa Field, Ewa Field, and Ford Island, most of the navy, army, and Marine Corps planes were only flaming wreckage by Sunday noon.

The 21 planes at Taranto sank or damaged seven Italian warships—3 planes per damaged ship. The 350 planes at Pearl Harbor sank or damaged fourteen warships—25 planes per damaged ship. Such a numerical comparison has limitations, but it could be said that the British pilots were eight times more efficient than their Japanese counterparts.

Factored into this numerical comparison should be the the the Swordfish's age and slowness, and the full-alert status of the Italian gun crews that met the British, as opposed to the somnolence of Pearl Harbor. In significance and efficiency, the Fleet Air Arm strike at Taranto merits at least the same historical prominence as Pearl Harbor.

In the wake of Taranto, Andrew B. Cunningham was promoted to full admiral in January 1941. In March, he led the fleet in a major victory at the Battle of Cape Matapan. By May, the tide had turned against the British; the Nazis had captured Greece and Crete, and the next twelve months consisted of merely holding on and enduring. From June to October 1942, Cunningham headed the British Admiralty delegation to the American Combined Chiefs of Staff. He so impressed Gen. Dwight D. Eisenhower that the American insisted that ABC be the naval person covering the landings in northern Africa, Sicily, and Salerno. When Italy surrendered, Cunningham sent the historic signal, "Be pleased to inform Their Lordships that the Italian battle fleet now lies at anchor beneath the guns of the Fortress of Malta." In January 1943, he resumed his post of commander in chief, Mediterranean, and was promoted to admiral of the fleet. Later the same year, he was appointed first sea lord and chief of naval staff, posts he held for the remainder of the war. In 1945, he was made Baron Cunningham of Hyndhope and in the following year was elevated to Viscount Cunningham. In his retirement, he authored an autobiography and served as high commissioner to the General Assembly of the Church of Scotland. Cunningham died in London in 1963 and was buried at sea.

Adm. Arturo Riccardi, base commander at Taranto, had often expressed concern at the coordination of the antiaircraft defenses around the harbor.

Taranto Night confirmed his worst fears. On December 8, 1940, he received his new orders. Perhaps to his surprise, he was promoted to chief of naval staff. Riccardi survived the war, in administrative assignments.

Admiral Yamamoto, the architect of success at Pearl Harbor, seems to have known from the outset that the course dictated by the Japanese Army, that of confronting the United States, was folly. In November 1941 he wrote to his old friend, retired admiral Teikichi Hori. In that letter, he concluded: "What a strange position I find myself in now—having to make a decision diametrically opposed to my own personal opinion with no choice but to push full ahead in pursuance of that decision. Is that, too, fate? And what a bad start we have made, with one serious accident after another, resulting from blunders from the very beginning of the year."

Following Pearl Harbor, Yamamoto's attempt to destroy the U.S. carrier fleet was a disaster. Two months later, in a series of piecemeal naval battles near Guadalcanal, Yamamoto lost many destroyers and most of his trained pilots and gained very little.

In April 1943, U.S. naval intelligence intercepted and decoded a message that Yamamoto would be flying to confer with his commanders near the island of Bougainville. Maj. John Mitchell of the U.S. Army Air Corps, leading a flight of sixteen P-38 Lightnings and navigating with only an airspeed indicator, his wristwatch, and a compass installed the night before, flew 450 miles over open water and made an exact interception of Yamamoto's plane. Around noon on April 18, 1943, Yamamoto died at the controls of one of the Betty bombers whose development he had promoted. Following a state funeral in Tokyo, his ashes were interred next to those of Admiral Togo, his mentor and inspiration.

The carriers that survived Taranto and Pearl Harbor have their own stories to tell. Hitler, annoyed at the ineffectiveness of the Regia Aeronautica, sent Fliegerkorps X to Sicily with Stuka dive-bombers, twin-engine JU-88 dive-bombers, long-range fighters, and long-range reconnaissance planes. On January 7, 1941, this force pounced on the *Illustrious* and put seven 1,000-pound bombs through her decks, plus five misses near enough to damage the hull. The ship was swept by fire and the steering mechanism disabled, but in a few hours she was able to make enough steam to get up to fourteen knots and to enter the harbor at Malta. Eighty-three of her crew were killed in the bombing attack. In spite of more air raids and further damage while in harbor, repairs enabled the ship to navigate to Alexandria on the night of January 23, from where she made her way through the Suez Canal, around Africa, and across the Atlantic Ocean to Norfolk, Virginia, where she underwent extensive repairs. After the war, she served as a training vessel for nine years and in 1956 was broken up for scrap.

The *Eagle's* aircraft, during her 1940 repairs at Alexandria, operated in the western desert under 201 Group, RAF. With the Suez Canal closed by Axis bombing, the *Eagle* was unable to enter the Red Sea until April 1941. Her planes, which had flown ahead, busied themselves with attacks on the Italians at Massawa, until their carrier caught up with them and, in early May, began hunting subs and raiders in the South Atlantic. She later traveled to the United Kingdom for a much-needed full refit, then returned to the Mediterranean where, on August 11, 1942, the German submarine U-73 put four torpedoes into her port side. In four minutes, she rolled over and sank, and 160 of her crew were lost.

The *Hermes* was with Admiral Somerville's Indian Ocean Fleet in the spring following Pearl Harbor. Sixty-five miles from Ceylon, on April 5, 1942, she and her three escorts were attacked by Japanese dive-bombers and sunk.

The *Furious* survived the war unscathed and was broken up for scrap in 1948. The *Courageous* was hit by two torpedoes from U-29 and sank in fifteen minutes. The *Glorious* was sunk by the battle cruisers *Scharnhorst* and *Gneisenau*. *Ark Royal* was hit by a single torpedo from U-81, which opened a hole 130 feet long and 30 feet high. Electric power to the pumps failed, and she sank fourteen hours later.

The Japanese aircraft carriers *Kaga, Akagi, Soryu,* and *Hiryu* went down at Midway; *Ryujo* was sunk in the Battle of the Eastern Solomons; *Shokaku* was lost in the Philippine Sea; *Zuikaku* and *Zuiho* were sunk at the Battle of Cape Engano; and *Shoho* sank at the Battle of the Coral Sea.

The canvas-covered Fairey Swordfish seemed to be more durable than the armored ships. Swordfish were still flying at the end of the war, off tiny Merchant Aircraft Carrier (MAC) ships, and the last one was retired from active service in 1946. Two Stringbags still fly, in the Royal Naval Historic Flight. One is W5984, to represent the aircraft flown by Lieutenant Commander Esmond, who was killed in an attack on the *Scharnhorst* and *Gneisenau*. The other is W5856 and was rebuilt by British Aerospace in 1992–93.

And of the men who flew at Taranto? It is customary for nations to honor heroic deeds. After the outpouring of praise that followed the attack, there was surprise and dismay when awards were given only to a few. The Royal Navy followed the policy that the crews were trained to do a job, and if they did that job, that should be enough. The December 20, 1940, supplement to the *London Gazette* announced that the DSO had been awarded to the two strike leaders, Lieutenant Commanders N. W. Williamson and J. W. Hale, and the DSC to their two observers, Lieutenants N. J. Scarlett and G. A. Carline, and to Capt. O. Patch, Royal Marines, and his observer, Lt. D. J. Goodwin. There the list ended. There was some ill feeling, both on aircraft carriers and in high circles, and a later list added more decorations. But whatever ribbons and medals a government may or may not award, the bravery and skill of those fliers, and all those who provided for their needs and tended their machines, cannot be diminished.

Britain's success at Taranto derived from the skill and fortitude of the pilots and observers, the hard work of the aircraft maintenance crews, the careful staff work from 1935 onward that resulted in the final plan, and the coordinated efforts that defeated aerial reconaissance by the Regia Aeronautica. Contributing to Italy's defeat were the internal political struggles that deprived the Italian Navy of effective scouting aircraft capable of finding an enemy and staying airborne long enough to report the discovery. The poor marksmanship of the gunners (not unusual in 1940), who fired 7,000 rounds for each British plane shot down, was another factor, although in the harbor of Taranto there was certainly alertness on the part of the antiaircraft batteries.

At Pearl Harbor, noteworthy were the thorough intelligence studies, intensive training, and determined pressing home of the attack by Japanese naval forces, as well as the remarkably quick reactions of the U.S. Navy enlisted men and junior officers, who shot down twenty-nine Japanese planes in spite of a serious lack of leadership by senior officers. Japan failed in neglecting to bomb the American fuel depot and the naval repair facilities, either of which would have forced the U.S. Navy back to California. But worst of all was the American failure to anticipate the attack, a failure that has been the subject of numerous investigations and dozens of books, examining the role of code breaking, conspiracies, and possible duplicity at the highest levels. Some authors are convinced that further answers will come when the last of Churchill's secret papers are unsealed. Nevertheless, much can be learned by the examination of well-documented historic antecedents.

The real surprise is that the American commanders were surprised. Both professional and lay journals had predicted a Japanese attack for more than forty-three years. The United States had "attacked" Pearl Harbor twice in fleet exercises, and perhaps most significant, in Taranto the British had shown how to do it in actual combat, in a shallow harbor, against an alerted enemy, and only thirteen months earlier, an event reported on the front pages of nearly every newspaper in the world.

One of the authors (Wellham), based on his long experience as a naval officer and on many Staff College discussions with U.S. Navy and Royal Navy colleagues, who had access to intelligence information, draws the following conclusions:

After Taranto, the U.S. chiefs of staff were warned by intelligence officers of at least three nations that the Japanese were studying Taranto and had visited that harbor. The U.S. chiefs of staff had been warned of the torpedo practice at Kagoshima, which resembles Pearl Harbor. The U.S. chiefs of staff knew that Japanese spies had been photographing Pearl Harbor. The Japanese carrier fleet was known to be somewhere at sea in late November, maintaining radio silence. The Congress had little sympathy for the British, and the U.S. public favored neutrality, but Roosevelt strongly supported the British side. Only an attack on a peacetime America would create a situation that would bring fame to the chiefs of staff before their retirements and allow Roosevelt to give Churchill the full support that both longed for. A "blameless" entry into the war, bought at the cost of a few obsolete battleships (the carriers were not in harbor) and a few thousand men, was cheap at the price.

The other author (Lowry) favors a somewhat different conclusion, based in part on thirty-five years of professional listening to human self-delusion and in part on historical studies such as Barbara Tuchman's *The March to Folly.* In the 1930s in America, the low prestige of military service and the slow advancement in the peacetime army and navy almost guaranteed that most of those in effective power would be bound by rigid traditions and foolish interservice rivalries and slowed by age. How else to explain the almost somnambulistic pace of antiaircraft preparation, the lack of appreciation of the Battle of Britain, the utter failure to send patrol planes to the north, the truly astounding failure to comprehend the lesson of Taranto, the petty foolishness of locking ammunition chests, and in Washington, the lunatic practice of giving the army and navy the responsibility of carrying intelligence to the White House on alternate days? Plain human foolishness, compounded by an arrogant feeling of racial superiority, seems the best explanation.

The noted historian Samuel Eliot Morison was adamantly opposed to the concept of a Roosevelt–chiefs of staff conspiracy, which made Kimmel and Short into sacrificial lambs. Morison wrote, in 1963, that the fault was "the inability to imagine" that Japan would do anything so suicidal. Morison describes at length the administrative mismanagement of intelligence information and the ludicrous division of responsibility, and concluded that "sins of omission" were the culprit.[10]

Henry C. Clausen, by profession a prosecuting attorney, was in 1945 one of the chief investigators of Pearl Harbor. Clausen is much less kind. In his summation to the jury of history, Clausen assigns culpability on a scale of one to ten, ten being the worst. He assigns Lt. Gen. Walter C. Short and Adm. Husband E. Kimmel both tens as fully guilty of neglect of duty. Col. Carlisle C. Dusenberg, in Army Intelligence in Washington, D.C., rated a nine for his failure to deliver crucial decryptions to Gen. George Marshall. Four men rated an eight, including Rear Adm. Richmond K. Turner, whom Clausen found guilty of contributory negligence for his misguided obstruction of intelligence data. Six men were rated a six or a seven on the culpability scale, while Roosevelt is rated a five for his contributory negligence, not because of leading a conspiracy, but for failure to exercise leadership at a crucial moment.[11]

Racism further intensified the conflicts. The Japanese culture, homogeneous for centuries, regarded all others as outsiders. The Caucasian colonists could not believe that Asiatics were to be taken seriously, no matter what the evidence to the contrary. But Japan's expansionist policies were in inevitable conflict with American, British, French, and Dutch colonial holdings. A collision was unavoidable; only the specifics were unknown.

That the naval base at Pearl Harbor was essential to American defense of the Pacific was recognized by both sides. Before Taranto, an attack on Pearl Harbor was only a classroom exercise for Japanese officers. Afterward, it was the example that proved the vulnerability of the U.S. Pacific Fleet.

Taranto was truly the blueprint for Pearl Harbor.

# Appendix A

➤

# British Naval Aviation

THE SUCCESSFUL ATTACK ON TARANTO WAS THE CULMINATION OF THIRTY-two years of dedication, determination, and painstaking practice by Royal Navy air crews. Naval aviation in Britain was born in July 1908, when the Admiralty created a new post, naval air assistant. Early flying was based on lighter-than-air craft, such as dirigibles and blimps. Such craft were vulnerable to gusts of wind, however, and Rigid Naval Aircraft No. 1 was totally destroyed in September 1911 when being taken out of its shed.

The first naval officer to learn to fly an aeroplane was Lt. G. C. Colmore, who learned at his own expense and was awarded Aviator's Certificate No. 15 on June 21, 1910. The third Royal Navy officer to fly was Lt. A. M. Longmore, later to be Air Chief Marshal Sir Arthur Longmore.

In 1910, it was less than seven years since the Wright brothers had first flown. Pilots could not fly on gusty days, and damp air was thought to have no "lift." When the coveted aviator's certificate was granted in those days, the new graduate had less flying experience than would be considered today for a first solo flight.

Barely trained, with a mixture of half lunacy and half courage, early pilots attempted feats such as landing on a platform bolted to a gun turret. In a naval service, it is not surprising that the initial emphasis was on airplanes that could arise from the sea. This was achieved in November 1911, when Comdr. Oliver Schwann succeeded in lifting off the water, flying an Avro biplane. In May 1912, Lt. C. R. Samson achieved a first when he took off from HMS *Hibernia,* while she was steaming at ten knots.

It soon became clear, however, that the seaplane had many disadvantages. The pontoons introduced tremendous drag; the planes could not land when the seas were rough; and when operating with the fleet, there were long delays while aircraft were being launched or recovered. Nevertheless, until nearly the end of the First World War, seaplanes were the only aircraft operating from ships, and they acquitted themselves with some distinction.

On May 13, 1912, the Royal Flying Corps was founded, with separate naval and military wings. The idea of being part of another unit did not please the Royal Navy, which had long been accepted as the Senior Service. In fact, the Articles of War clearly stated that the defense of the realm principally depended "upon the navy under the good Providence of God." This resulted in the title Royal Naval Air Service being adopted almost immediately, if not officially.

At the outbreak of hostilities in 1914, the Royal Naval Air Service had seventy-eight aircraft, including seven lighter-than-air ships. Of a total of 170 personnel, 100 were trained pilots. As soon as war began, the Royal Flying Corps was fully occupied over the western front in France and Belgium, and the Royal Naval Air Service was given the responsibility for the air defense of Great Britain, not only over the Channel, but over the land itself.

The original aircraft carriers would stop at sea, lower the seaplanes over the side with a crane or roll them down a sloping platform, and recover them in the same way. The concept of launching and recovering a wheeled plane from a flat deck was very slow to develop. It was not until 1918 that the first fully decked carrier, HMS *Argus,* entered service.

By the end of the war, twenty-two light cruisers and all battleships were equipped with takeoff platforms, but none had any way of recovering their planes.

The Avro 504, which first appeared in 1913 and stayed in service until the early 1930s, was unusually versatile. In October 1914, three of them, led by Squadron Comdr. E. F. Briggs, took off from Belfort, near the Franco-Swiss border; flew north of Basel, along the Rhine; then crossed Lake Constance, skimming over the water to avoid detection. They climbed to 1,200 feet, then dived onto the German Zeppelin sheds at Friedrichshafen, launching their tiny twenty-pound bombs. One Zeppelin was severely damaged, and the gas-producing facility was hit, hurling flames high into the air. This attack was a marvelous achievement of navigation, in planes with no instruments, flying 250 miles over enemy territory through heavy gunfire. The following year, five Avro 504s attacked the German submarine base at Hoboken, set the shipyard on fire, and destroyed two submarines.

The concept of long-range night air raids on enemy territory came, surprisingly, from the navy rather than from the army. Commodore Murray Suiter, with typical naval brevity, requested a "bloody paralyzer of an airplane." This resulted in the enormous Handley Page 0/100, which had a wingspan of 100 feet and a length of 63 feet. It could carry almost 700 pounds of bombs, and made attacks on Constantinople, Cologne, and Mannheim.

In spite of the obvious advantages of the land planes, many World War I seaplanes achieved distinction. The outstanding British seaplane design was the Short Type 184. In 1915, 184s torpedoed three Turkish ships, a historic first.

Flying boats, such as the versatile Felixtowe F-2A, and blimps were widely used along the coast for antisubmarine work. When the war came to an end, the Royal Naval Air Service had grown to 67,000 officers and men, 2,949 aeroplanes, 103 airships, and 126 air stations.

In 1918, complex political maneuvering resulted in the merger of the Royal Flying Corps and the Royal Naval Air Serice into a wholly new organization, the Royal Air Force. The naval side became the Fleet Air Arm of the RAF. Naval aviation came under the command of land-based administrators, who cared little about naval matters, and ship captains, who cared little about aviation. (By contrast, the U.S. Navy not only kept a separate Naval Air Service, but in 1926, Congress mandated that all captains of aircraft carriers and commanders of air bases be qualified aviators. This resulted in such remarkable occurrences as the future Adm. William F. Halsey returning to flying school at age fifty-five.)

A slight political remediation of the RAF's infringement upon naval aviation was achieved in 1923, when it was agreed that the navy would provide all the observers in naval aircraft and that 70 percent of all pilots should be naval officers holding joint Royal Air Force rank. Until 1937, no ship designed from the start as a carrier was in service; all carriers were conversions from other types. When the *Ark Royal* entered service in 1938, she was the first Royal Navy ship designed from the keel up as a carrier.

The Royal Navy tradition that gunnery is the basis of maritime warfare also hampered aviation. In the 1930s, the navy was administered by the Admiralty, which was ruled by gentlemen who held the grandiose title of the Lords Commissioners for Executing the Office of Lord High Admiral. This board of five men consisted of the First Sea Lord, who was a political appointee, and four sea lords who were admirals. These men believed in battleships, and it was not until well into World War II, with British and Italian battleships being sunk by airborne torpedoes, that ideas began to change.

In 1937, a momentous political decision was made to return naval aviation to the navy, this change to take place over a two-year period. The navy's reaction was immediate and positive. Officers of the RAF were offered commissions in the Royal Navy with the equivalent rank. Maintenance personnel were transferred from the RAF, and naval personnel were trained. Recruiting for pilots and observers commenced, and a volunteer reserve was formed.

It was very late in the game, however. When the Admiralty finally took full control, the outbreak of war was only three months away. At that time, the navy had only 340 aircraft, almost entirely biplanes. Japanese and American naval planes were more advanced, designed in a different administrative culture. Thus, in the three months that remained before the outbreak of the war, the Royal Navy had far too little time for the political, psychological, aeronautical, and educational changes needed to make best use of those men who wore wings on navy blue.

# *Appendix B*

## ➤

# The Raid on Bomba

THREE MONTHS BEFORE TARANTO, A BRIEF ENCOUNTER ON THE LIBYAN coast greatly influenced the British high command about the possibilities of airborne torpedoes.

Swordfish detached from the *Eagle* were sent to Ma'aten Bagush in the Western Desert, then the RAF headquarters; they were accompanied by an ancient Victoria transport plane, loaded with supplies and mechanics. Among the latter was Leading Torpedoman Arthey, who could keep a delicate "fish" running in a desert of blowing sand.

After two nights of fruitless patrolling, the dusk patrol reported Italian ships in Bomba Bay, between Tobruk and Benghazi. Around 6:00 A.M., Capt. Oliver Patch, Royal Marines, arrived by air and took command. The three Swordfish were loaded with torpedoes and departed for the airfield at Sidi Barrâni, ninety minutes to the west and pocked with bomb craters. After landing safely, they refueled, ate a breakfast of canned sausages and baked beans, and heard the dawn report: There were still ships at Bomba.

At 10:38 A.M., Captain Patch, with his observer Midshipman (Acting) C. J. Woodley, led the other two westward. The port aircraft was piloted by Lt. (Acting) J. W. G. Wellham, with P.O. A. H. Marsh as observer. The starboard craft was flown by Lt. (Acting) N. A. F. Cheesman, with Sub-lieutenant F. Stovin-Bradford as observer.

They flew fifty miles off the coast until 12:30, then turned inshore. Woodley's navigation was perfect: There was Bomba Bay. The three planes spread out to 200 yards apart. Suddenly a submarine appeared in front of Patch. Its crew fired both machine guns at Patch until they saw the splash of his torpedo; then they dived overboard and began to swim. The torpedo struck. The submarine disappeared, and Patch turned for home.

The other two planes flew on. They saw three ships, lying side by side: a sub-tender, a destroyer, and a second submarine. Alerted by Patch's torpedo, they were already firing pom-poms at the two Swordfish. Wellham launched his torpedo at the starboard beam of the destroyer.

Cheesman's observer saw that the water was too shallow for launching, and he was forced to fly within 250 yards of the warships before launching. The two torpedoes struck within three seconds of each other. The submarine exploded, setting fire to the tender, which also exploded, taking the crippled destroyer with it. In a minute, they were all gone. By 3:00 P.M., all three planes were back at Sidi Barrâni, having sunk four ships with three torpedoes. The British damage consisted of two bullet holes in Wellham's plane. Italian radio reported that an overwhelming force had attacked their fleet.

One of the submarines was the *Iride,* carrying three manned torpedoes, destined for the British battleships at Alexandria. The three Swordfish may have saved three battleships, since a later such attack at Alexandria sank the battleships *Valiant* and *Queen Elizabeth* and the tanker *Sagona,* and badly damaged the destroyer *Jervis.* Wellham received the Distinguished Service Cross.

*Appendix C*

➤

# Flight Crews at Taranto

## FIRST WAVE

| Aircraft number | Pilot and Observer |
|---|---|
| L4A | Lt. Cdr. K. Williamson, R.N. <br> Lt. N. J. Scarlett, R.N. |
| L4C | Sub Lt. P. D. J. Sparke, D.S.C., R.N. <br> Sub Lt. A. L. O. Neale, R.N. |
| L4R | Sub Lt. A. S. D. Macaulay, R.N. <br> Sub Lt. A. L. O. Wray, R.N.V.R. |
| L4K | Lt. N. M. Kemp, R.N. <br> Sub Lt. R. A. Bailey, R.N. |
| L4M | Lt. H. A. I. Swayne, R.N. <br> Sub Lt. J. Buscall, R.N.V.R. |
| E4F | Lt. M. R. Maund, R.N. <br> Sub Lt. W.A. Bull, R.N. |
| L4P | Lt. L. J. Kiggell, R.N. <br> Lt. H. R. B. Janvrin, R.N. |
| L5B | Lt. C. B. Lamb, R.N. <br> Lt. K. C. Grieve, R.N. |

| | |
|---|---|
| E5A | Capt. O. Patch, R.M.<br>Lt. D. G. Goodwin, R.N. |
| L4L | Sub Lt. W. C. Sarra, R.N.<br>Mid. J. Bowker, R.N. |
| L4H | Sub Lt. A. J. Forde, R.N.<br>Sub Lt. A. Mardel–Ferreira, R.N.V.R. |
| E5Q | Lt. J. B. Murray, R.N.<br>Sub Lt. S. M. Paine, R.N. |

## SECOND WAVE

| | |
|---|---|
| L5A | Lt. Cdr. J. W. Hale, R.N.<br>Lt. G. A. Carline, R.N. |
| E4H | Lt. G. W. Bayley, R.N.<br>Lt. H. J. Slaughter, R.N. |
| L5H | Lt. C. S. C. Lea, R.N.<br>Sub Lt. P. D. Jones, R.N. |
| L5K | Lt. F. M. A. Torrens-Spence, R.N.<br>Lt. A. W. F. Sutton, R.N. |
| E5H | Lt. J. W. G. Wellham, R.N.<br>Lt. P. Humphreys, E.G.M., R.N. |
| L5B | Lt. R. W. V. Hamilton, R.N.<br>Sub Lt. J. R. Weeks, R.N. |
| L4F | Lt. R. G. Skelton, R.N.<br>Sub Lt. E. A. Perkins, R.N.V.R. |
| L5F | Lt. E. W. Clifford, R.N.<br>Lt. G. R. M. Going, R.N. |
| L5Q | Lt. W. D. Morford, R.N.<br>Sub Lt. R. A. F. Green, R.N. |

➤

# Italian Naval Ships at Taranto

## IN THE MAR GRANDE

| **Battleships** | **Cruisers** | **Destroyers** |
|---|---|---|
| *Vittorio Veneto* | *Zara* | *Folgare* |
| *Littorio* | *Fiume* | *Baleno* |
| *Cavour* | *Gorizia* | *Fulmine* |
| *Giulio Cesare* | | *Lampo* |
| *Caio Duilio* | | *A. Gioberti* |
| *Andrea Doria* | | *Carducci* |
| | | *Oriani* |

## IN THE MAR PICCOLO

**Cruisers**

*Trieste*
*Bolzano*
*Pola*
*Trento*
*Garibaldi*
*Abruzzi*

Also in the Mar Piccolo:
   Sixteen submarines
   Five torpedo boats
   Four minesweepers
   Nine tankers
   One minelayer
   Two hospital ships

**Destroyers**

| | |
|---|---|
| *Granatiere* | *Scirocco* |
| *Alpino* | *Camicia Nera* |
| *Bersagliere* | *Geniere* |
| *Fuciliere* | *Lanciere* |
| *Freccia* | *Carabiniere* |
| *Strale* | *Corazziere* |
| *Dardo* | *Ascari* |
| *Saetta* | *Da Recco* |
| *Maestrale* | *Usodimare* |
| *Libeccio* | *Pessagno* |
| *Grecale* | |

≻

# Maximum Speeds of Planes in Use in 1940–41

In miles per hour, level flight at 5,000 feet.

| Name | Type | MPH | Knots |
|------|------|-----|-------|
| Messerschmitt 109 | fighter | 354 | 308 |
| Supermarine Seafire | fighter | 352 | 306 |
| Mitsubishi A6M3 Zero | fighter | 339 | 295 |
| Macchi-200 | fighter | 318 | 277 |
| Fairey Firefly | fighter/reconnaissance | 316 | 275 |
| Hawker Hurricane | fighter | 300 | 261 |
| Savoia-Marchetti 79 | bomber | 280 | 244 |
| Martin Maryland | bomber | 278 | 242 |
| Fiat CR-42 | fighter | 275 | 239 |
| Fairey Fulmar | fighter | 272 | 237 |
| Grumman TBF Avenger | torpedo | 271 | 236 |
| Gloster Gladiator | fighter | 253 | 220 |
| Heinkel 111 | bomber | 252 | 219 |
| Aichi D3A1 (Val) | dive-bomber | 239 | 208 |
| Nakajima B5N2 (Kate) | dive/torpedo | 235 | 204 |
| Fairey Barracuda | torpedo | 228 | 198 |

| Name | Type | MPH | Knots |
|------|------|-----|-------|
| Blackburn Skua | fighter/bomber | 220 | 191 |
| Cant Z-506 | reconnaissance/torpedo | 217 | 189 |
| Short Sunderland | flying boat | 210 | 183 |
| Blackburn Roc | fighter | 196 | 171 |
| Cant Z-501 | flying boat/reconnaissance | 170 | 148 |
| Fairey Albacore | torpedo/dive | 161 | 140 |
| Fairey Swordfish | torpedo/dive | 154 | 134 |
| Supermarine Walrus | flying boat | 124 | 108 |

*Though many characteristics besides speed are relevant, all things being equal, the faster plane has an advantage. Not all printed sources agree regarding top speeds of a particular plane.*

## Appendix F

### ➤

# Midway

IN EARLY MAY 1942, NAVY INTELLIGENCE WAS FAIRLY CERTAIN THAT THE Japanese would attack Midway around June 4. There remained the possibility, however, that either the main blow, or a diversionary one, might be directed at San Francisco.

On very short notice, a number of private sailboats and their owners were asked to volunteer for picket duty, to sail back and forth several hundred miles off the coast looking for Yamamoto's fleet. They were provided with a navy radioman and a suitable radio for sending a warning. An ensign with a rifle was to provide a military presence. It was understood that any yacht spotting the Japanese fleet would be almost certainly sunk as soon as the Japanese detected the American radio signals.

Most of the navy men were new to the ocean and spent the duration of the voyage in their bunks vomiting. The navy supplies handed out were more adapted to a battleship than to a yawl or ketch, and included sides of beef and live chickens.

A gale came down out of the Gulf of Alaska, green water crashed over the cockpits, and many of the boats ran under bare poles or a small storm trysail until the storm abated. Only one boat came in from the storm, to unload two navy men on the verge of death from days of retching.

On one yacht, the nausea-befuddled ensign took his noon sighting and calculated that they were just north of Mexico City even though they were off Cape Mendocino in northern California. On another vessel, the cook provided by the navy had yet to go to cooking school, but learned on the job as his galley heaved and pitched. Since no one had thought to provide the sailboats with the password, one was attacked by a plane, fortunately without harm.

The civilian volunteers, who had small-boat experience, survived the ordeal with less suffering than their uniformed comrades. Of course, we know now that they saw no Japanese ships. But they could have.

(Richard Lowry, one author's father, was a volunteer on the cutter *Water Witch*.)

# Appendix G

>

# Comparative Ranks

| Regia Aeronautica | Royal Air Force | Luftwaffe |
|---|---|---|
| Colonnello | Group Captain | Oberst |
| Tenente Colonnelo | Wing Commander | Oberstleutnant |
| Maggiore | Squadron Leader | Major |
| 1° Capitano | Flight Lieutenant | Hauptmann |
| Capitano | | |
| 1° Tenente | Flying Officer | Oberleutnant |
| Tenente | | |
| Sottotenente | Pilot Officer | Leutnant |
| Maresciallo Maggiore | Warrant Officer | |
| Maresciallo Capo | | Stabsfeldwebel |
| Sergent Maggiore | Flight Sergeant | Oberfeldwebel |
| Sergent | Sergeant | Unterfeldwebel |
| Primo Aviere | Leading Airman | Unteroff |

# Comparative Ranks (continued)

| U.S. Army Air Corps | Royal Navy |
|---|---|
| Colonel | Captain |
| Lieutenant Colonel | Commander |
| Major | Lieutenant Commander |
| Captain | Lieutenant |
| First Lieutenant | Sub-Lieutenant |
| Second Lieutenant | Midshipman |
| Chief Warrant Officer | Warrant Officer |
| Warrant Officer | |
| Master Sergeant | Chief Petty Officer |
| Technical Sergeant | Petty Officer |

# Appendix H

>

# British Abbreviations

| | |
|---|---|
| AFC | Air Force Cross |
| CBE | Companion of the British Empire |
| DSC | Distinguished Service Cross |
| DSO | Distinguished Service Order |
| OBE | Order of the British Empire |
| RAF | Royal Air Force |
| RMA | Royal Military Academy |
| RNR | Royal Naval Reserve |
| RN | Royal Navy |
| VRD | Volunteer Reserve Decoration |

# Notes

➤

## CHAPTER ONE

1. William Jameson, *Ark Royal 1939–1941* (London: Rupert Hart-Davis, 1957), 134.

## CHAPTER TWO

1. Viscount Cunningham of Hyndhope, *A Sailor's Odyssey* (London: Hutchinson, 1951), 70.
2. Max Gallo, *Mussolini's Italy* (New York: Macmillan, 1973), 316.
3. William H. Honan, *Visions of Infamy* (New York: St. Martin's Press, 1991), 10.
4. Hiroyuki Agawa, *Reluctant Admiral: Yamamoto of the Imperial Japanese Navy* (San Francisco: Kodansha, 1982), 74.
5. Honan, *Visions of Infamy*, 19.
6. Ibid., 70.
7. Ibid., 272.
8. Ibid., 194.
9. Ibid., 225.
10. Clark G. Reynolds, *The Carrier War* (Alexandria, VA: Time-Life Books, 1982), 33.
11. Norman Polmar, *Aircraft Carriers* (New York: Doubleday, 1969), 54.
12. Reynolds, *The Carrier War*, 34.
13. Polmar, *Aircraft Carriers*, 58.
14. Ibid., 60.
15. John Deane Potter, *Admiral of the Pacific* (London: Heinemann, 1965), 48; Ladislas Farago, *The Broken Seal* (New York: Random House, 1967), 127.
16. Agawa, *Reluctant Admiral*, 193.
17. Polmar, *Aircraft Carriers*, 60.

## CHAPTER THREE

1. Bernard Fitzsimons, *The Illustrated Encyclopedia of 20th Century Weapons & Warfare* (New York: Columbia House, 1977), 2441.

2. Leonard Bridgman, ed., *Jane's All the World's Aircraft* (New York: Macmillan, 1941), 22c.

3. John W. G. Wellham, personal recollection, 1940.

4. Terence Horsley, *Find, Fix and Strike* (London: Eyre and Spottiswoode, 1943), 22.

### CHAPTER FOUR

1. Norman Polmar, *Aircraft Carriers* (New York: Doubleday, 1969), 28.

2. Clark G. Reynolds, *The Carrier War* (Alexandria, VA: Time-Life Books, 1982), 28.

3. *Conway's All the World's Fighting Ships, 1922–1946* (London: Conway's Maritime Press, 1980), 19.

4. Gordon Wallace, *Carrier Observer* (Shrewsbury, England: Airlife Publishing, 1993), 85.

5. William Jameson, *Ark Royal 1939–1941* (London: Rupert Hart-Davis, 1957), 10.

6. Edwyn Gray, *The Devil's Device* (London: Seeley-Service, 1975), 40.

7. *Encyclopedia Brittanica,* 1911 ed., s.v. "torpedo."

8. Ronald H. Spector, *Eagle against the Sun* (New York: Vintage Books, 1985), 161.

9. Gray, *Devil's Device,* 224

10. John W. G. Wellham, personal recollection, 1994.

11. Donald M. Goldstein, personal communication, 1991.

12. Gordon W. Prange, *At Dawn We Slept* (New York: McGraw-Hill, 1981), 329.

### CHAPTER FIVE

1. A. B. C. Whipple, *The Mediterranean* (Alexandria, VA: Time-Life Books, 1981), 12.

2. William H. Honan, *Visions of Infamy* (New York: St. Martin's Press, 1991), 215.

3. *Conway's All the World's Fighting Ships: 1922–1946* (London: Conway's Maritime Press, 1980), 280; John Jordan, *Illustrated Guide to Battleships and Battle Cruisers* (New York: Arco Publishing, 1985), 84.

4. *Conway's All the World's Fighting Ships,* 284.

5. Ibid., 281; ibid., 285.

6. Hugh Gibson, *The Ciano Diaries, 1939–1943* (New York: Doubleday, 1946), 247; Max Gallo, *Mussolini's Italy* (New York: Macmillan, 1973), 318.

7. Marc' Antonio Bragadin, *The Italian Navy in World War II* (New York: Ayer Publishing, 1980), 20.

8. Ibid., 8.

9. Viscount Cunningham of Hyndhope, *A Sailor's Odyssey* (London: Hutchinson, 1951), 89.

10. Leonard Bridgman, ed., *Jane's All the World's Aircraft* (New York: Macmillan, 1941), 49.

11. Angelo Del Boca, *The Ethiopian War, 1935–1941* (Chicago: University of Chicago Press, 1960), 92.

12. Christopher Shores, *Regia Aeronautica, vol. 1* (Carrollton, TX: Squadron/Signal Publications, 1976), 5.

13. Chris Dunning, *Combat Units of the Regia Aeronautica, Italian Air Force 1940–1943,* (Oxford: Oxford University Press, 1988), 7.

## CHAPTER SIX

1. Ernle Bradford, *Siege: Malta 1940–1943* (New York: William Morrow, 1986), 22.

2. Martin Windrow, *Aircraft in Profile, vol. 8* (New York: Doubleday, 1970), 292; Edward Jablonski, *Man with Wings* (New York: Doubleday, 1980), 222.

3. Owen Thetford, *Aircraft of the Royal Air Force since 1918* (London: Putnam, 1985), 422.

4. Christopher Shores and Brian Cull, *Malta: The Hurricane Years, 1940–1941* (London: Grub Street, 1987), 10.

5. Brian Betham Schofield, *The Attack on Taranto* (Annapolis, MD: U.S. Naval Institute Press, 1973), 24.

## CHAPTER SEVEN

1. Viscount Cunningham of Hyndhope, *A Sailor's Odyssey* (London: Hutchinson, 1951), 273.

2. Naval Staff College,"Operation MB8 including the Naval Air Attack on Taranto" (Naval Staff College, 1952, Mimeographed), 2.

3. Brian Betham Schofield, *The Attack on Taranto* (Annapolis, MD: U. S. Naval Institute Press, 1973), 26.

## CHAPTER EIGHT

1. Brian Betham Schofield, *The Attack on Taranto* (Annapolis, MD: U.S. Naval Institute Press, 1973), 32.

2. Naval Staff History, Second World War, *Selected Operations, Mediterranean, 1940, Battle Summary No. 10,* B.R. 1736 (6), Royal Navy, 1957, 36.

### CHAPTER NINE

1. Christopher Shores and Brian Cull, *Malta: The Hurricane Years, 1940–1941* (London: Grub Street, 1987), 83.
2. Marc' Antonio Bragadin, *The Italian Navy in World War II* (New York: Ayer Publishing, 1980), 130.
3. Shores and Cull, *Malta,* 84.
4. Brian Betham Schofield, *The Attack on Taranto* (Annapolis, MD: U.S. Naval Institute Press, 1973), 34.
5. Naval Staff College,"Operation MB8 including the Naval Air Attack on Taranto" (Naval Staff College, 1952, Mimeographed), 3.
6. Ibid., 2.

### CHAPTER TEN

1. Naval Staff History, Second World War, *Selected Operations, Mediterranean, 1940, Battle Summary No. 10,* B.R. 1736 (6) 1957.
2. Brian Betham Schofield, *The Attack on Taranto* (Annapolis, MD: U.S. Naval Insitute Press, 1973), 44.
3. Naval Staff History, 87.
4. Ibid., 89.
5. John W. G. Wellham, flight log and personal recollection.

### CHAPTER ELEVEN

1. Naval Staff History, Second World War, *Selected Operations, Mediterranean, 1940, Battle Summary No. 10,* B.R. 1736 (6) 1957, 49; Brian Betham Schofield, *The Attack on Taranto* (Annapolis, MD: U.S. Naval Institute, 1973), 59.
2. Schofield, *Attack on Taranto,* 53.
3. Hugh Gibson, ed., *The Ciano Diaries, 1939–1943* (New York: Doubleday, 1946), 310.
4. Christopher Shores and Brian Cull, *Malta: The Hurricane Years, 1940–1941* (London: Grub Street, 1987), 85.
5. John Deane Potter, *Admiral of the Pacific* (London: Heinemann, 1965), 53; Edwin P. Hoyt, *Japan's War* (New York: McGraw-Hill, 1986), 106; Gordon W. Prange, *At Dawn We Slept* (New York: McGraw-Hill, 1981), 320.

### CHAPTER TWELVE

1. Ladislas Farago, *The Broken Seal* (New York: Random House, 1967), 132.
2. Ibid., 134.

3. Gordon W. Prange, *At Dawn We Slept* (New York: McGraw-Hill, 1981), 64.
4. Farago, *Broken Seal,* 13.
5. James Rusbridger and Eric Nave, *Betrayal at Pearl Harbor* (New York: Summit, 1991), 130.
6. Prange, *At Dawn We Slept,* 93.
7. Ibid., 159.
8. Donald M. Goldstein, personal communation, 1991.
9. Gordon W. Prange, Donald M. Goldstein, and Katherine Dillon, *God's Samurai: Lead Pilot at Pearl Harbor* (Alexandria, VA: Brassey's, 1990), 306; Prange, *At Dawn We Slept,* 320.
10. Adm. Giuseppe Fioravanzo, "The Japanese Military Mission to Italy in 1941," *U.S. Naval Institute Proceedings* (January 1956), 24; Adm. Renato Sicurezza, personal communication, 1993.
11. Prange, *At Dawn We Slept,* 159.
12. Norman Polmar, *Aircraft Carriers* (New York: Doubleday, 1969), 135.
13. John Deane Potter, *Admiral of the Pacific* (London: Heinemann, 1965), 77; Farago, *Broken Seal,* 138.

## CHAPTER THIRTEEN

1. Samuel Eliot Morison, *The Two Ocean War* (Boston: Little, Brown, 1963), 147.
2. Ira Peck, *The Battle of Midway* (New York: Scholastic Books, 1976), 30.
3. Morison, *Two Ocean War,* 156.
4. Ibid., 158.

## CHAPTER FOURTEEN

1. Brian Betham Schofield, *The Attack on Taranto* (Annapolis, MD: U.S. Naval Institute Press, 1973), 32.
2. Gordon W. Prange, *At Dawn We Slept* (New York: McGraw-Hill, 1981), 523.
3. J. L. Mooney, ed., *Dictionary of American Naval Fighting Ships,* 8 vols. (Washington, DC: U.S. Naval Historical Division, 1981); James C. Fahey, *The Ships and Aircraft of the United States Fleet* (New York: Ships and Aircraft, 1941), 4–17.
4. Prange, *At Dawn We Slept,* 523.
5. Donald M. Goldstein and Katherine V. Dillon, *The Way It Was: Pearl Harbor, the Original Photographs* (New York: Macmillan, 1991), 153.
6. Steven Floray, curator of the USS *Arizona* Memorial, personal communication, 1994.

7. John W. G. Wellham, personal recollection, 1994.

8. Tokuya Takahashi, statement given to Squadron Leader D. S. Hamilton, RNZAF, 1945. Courtesy of Henry Sakaida, Temple City, CA, 1994.

9. Bob Diemert, personal communication, 1994. (Mr. Diemert, of Carmon, Manitoba, Canada, is a test pilot with many hours in a rebuilt Val dive-bomber.)

10. Samuel Eliot Morison, *The Two Ocean War* (Boston: Little, Brown, 1963), 69.

11. Henry C. Clausen and Bruce Lee, *Pearl Harbor: Final Judgement* (New York: Crown Publishers, 1992), 286.

# Bibliography

➤

## BOOKS

Adams, Henry. *Italy at War.* Alexandria, VA: Time-Life Books, 1982.

Agawa, Hiroyuke. *The Reluctant Admiral.* Tokyo: Kodansha, 1979.

Angelucci, Enzo. *The Rand McNally Encyclopedia of Military Aircraft 1941–1980.* New York: Military Press, 1983.

Baldwin, Hanson W. *The Crucial Years, 1939–1941.* New York: Harper & Row, 1976.

Bradford, Ernle. *Siege: Malta 1940–1943.* New York: William Morrow, 1986.

Bragadin, Marc' Antonio. *The Italian Navy in World War II.* New York: Ayer, 1980.

Bridgman, Leonard, ed. *Jane's All the World's Aircraft.* New York: Macmillan, 1941.

Chesneau, Roger. *Aircraft Carriers of the World.* London: Arms & Armour, 1984.

Churchill, Winston S. *Their Finest Hour.* Boston: Houghton-Mifflin, 1949.

Clausen, Henry C., and Bruce Lee. *Pearl Harbor: Final Judgement.* New York: Crown, 1992.

Collier, Basil. *The Defense of the United Kingdom.* London: Her Majesty's Stationery Office, 1957.

*Conway's All the World's Fighting Ships, 1922–1946.* London: Conway's Maritime Press, 1980.

Cunningham, Viscount of Hyndhope. *A Sailor's Odyssey.* London: Hutchinson, 1951.

Deighton, Len. *The Battle of Britain.* London: George Rainbird, 1980.

Del Boca, Angelo. *The Ethiopian War, 1935–1941.* Chicago: University of Chicago Press, 1970.

Dunning, Chris. *Combat Units of the Regia Aeronautica, Italian Air Force 1940–1943.* Oxford: Oxford University Press, 1988.

Farago, Ladislas. *The Broken Seal.* New York: Random House, 1967.

Fitzsimons, Bernard. *The Illustrated Encyclopedia of 20th Century Weapons and Warfare.* New York: Columbia House, 1977.

Francillon, R. J. *Japanese Aircraft of the Pacific War.* New York: Funk & Wagnalls, 1970.

Gallo, Max. *Mussolini's Italy.* New York: Macmillan, 1973.

Gibson, Hugh, ed. *The Ciano Diaries, 1939–1943.* New York: Doubleday, 1946.

Gilbert, James. *The World's Worst Aircraft.* New York: St. Martin's, 1976.

Goldstein, Donald M., and Katherine V. Dillon. *The Way It Was: Pearl Harbor, the Original Photographs.* New York: Macmillan, 1991.

Heritage, John. *The Wonderful World of Aircraft.* London: Octopus, 1980.

Honan, William H. *Visions of Infamy.* New York: St. Martin's, 1991.

Horsley, Terence. *Find, Fix and Strike.* London: Eyre and Spottiswoode, 1943.

Hoyt, Edwin P. *Japan's War.* New York: McGraw-Hill, 1986

———. *Yamamoto.* New York: McGraw-Hill, 1990.

Hunt, Leslie. *Veteran and Vintage Aircraft.* New York: Taplinger, 1970.

Jablonski, Edward. *Seawings: The Romance of Flying Boats.* New York: Doubleday, 1972.

———. *Man with Wings.* New York: Doubleday, 1980.

Jameson, William. *Ark Royal, 1939–1941.* London: Rupert Hart-Davis, 1957.

Joiner, Susan, ed. *Fighting Aircraft of World Wars One and Two.* New York: Crescent Books, 1976.

Jordan, John. *Illustrated Guide to Battleships & Battlecruisers.* New York: Arco, 1985.

Kennedy, Ludovic. *Menace.* London: Sidgewick & Jackson, 1979.

Mason, Francis. *Battle over Britain.* London: McWhirter Twins, 1969.

Minister of Information. *Fleet Air Arm.* London: His Majesty's Stationery Office, 1943.

Mondey, David. *Pictorial History of Aircraft.* Trenton: Chartwell, 1977.

Mondey, David, ed. *British Aircraft of World War II.* Middlesex: Temple, 1982.

Morison, Samuel Eliot. *The Two Ocean War.* Boston: Little, Brown, 1963.

Munson, Kenneth. *Warplanes of Yesteryear.* New York: Arco, 1966.

Peck, Ira. *The Battle of Midway.* New York: Scholastic Books, 1976.

Pimlott, John. *Pictorial History of Military Aircraft.* New York: Gallery, 1987.

Polmar, Norman. *Aircraft Carriers.* New York: Doubleday, 1969.

Potter, John Deane. *Fiasco.* New York: Stein & Day, 1970.

———. *Admiral of the Pacific.* London: Heinemann, 1965.

Prange, Gordon W. *At Dawn We Slept.* New York: McGraw-Hill, 1981.

———. *December 7, 1941.* New York: McGraw-Hill, 1988.

———. *Miracle at Midway.* New York: McGraw-Hill, 1982.

Prange, Gordon W., Donald M. Goldstein, and Katherine Dillon. *God's Samurai: Lead Pilot at Pearl Harbor.* Alexandria, VA: Brassey's, 1990.

Ramsey, Winston, ed. *The Blitz, Then and Now.* Vol. 2. London: Britain Prints International, 1988.

Reynolds, Clark G. *The Carrier War.* Alexandria, VA: Time-Life, 1982.

Rusbridger, James, and Eric Nave. *Betrayal at Pearl Harbor.* New York: Summit, 1991.

Schofield, Brian Betham. *The Attack on Taranto.* Annapolis, MD: U.S. Naval Institute Press, 1973.

Shores, Christopher. *Regia Aeronautica.* Vol. 1. Carrolton, TX: Squadron/Signal, 1976.

Shores, Christopher, and Brian Cull. *Malta: The Hurricane Years, 1940–1941.* London: Grub Street, 1987.

Smith, Peter C. *The Story of the Torpedo Bomber.* London: Almark, 1974.

Snyder, Louis L. *The War: A Concise History.* New York: Julian Messner, 1960.

Spaight, J. M. *The Battle of Britain, 1940.* London: Geoffrey Bles, 1941.

Spector, Ronald H. *Eagle against the Sun.* New York: Vintage, 1985.

Thetford, Owen. *Aircraft of the Royal Air Force since 1918.* London: Putnam, 1985.

———. *British Naval Aircraft since 1912.* London: Putnam Aeronautical, 1958.

Wallace, Gordon. *Carrier Observer.* Shrewsbury, England: Airlife, 1993.

Whipple, A. B. C. *The Mediterranean.* Alexandria, VA: Time-Life, 1981.

Windrow, Martin. *Aircraft in Profile.* Vol. 8. New York: Doubleday, 1970.

Zich, Arthur. *The Rising Sun.* Alexandria, VA: Time-Life, 1977.

## ARTICLES AND MANUSCRIPTS

Alston, Gwen. "Obituary." *Fleet Air Arm Officers Association News Sheet* 20 (October 1993): 27.

Emmott, N. W. "R.A.F.: The Impossible Dream." *U.S. Naval Institute Proceedings* 12 (December 1969): 26.

Field, James A. "Admiral Yamamoto." *U.S. Naval Institute Proceedings* 10 (October 1949): 1105.

Fioravanzo, Giuseppe. "The Japanese Military Mission to Italy in 1941." *U.S. Naval Institute Proceedings* 1 (January 1956): 24.

Goerner, Frederick A. "Why Pearl Harbor?" *San Francisco Chronicle, This World,* December 1, 1991.

Naval Staff History (Royal Navy), Second World War. *Selected Operations, Mediterranean, 1940, Battle Summary No. 10.* B.R. 1736 (6) 1957.

*Operation MB8 including the Naval Air Attack on Taranto.* Naval Staff College (Royal Navy), 1952. Mimeo.

# Index

➤